Family History Research
in San Diego California

Barbara Palmer

HERITAGE BOOKS
2006

HERITAGE BOOKS
AN IMPRINT OF HERITAGE BOOKS, INC.

Books, CDs, and more   Worldwide

For our listing of thousands of titles see our website
at
www.HeritageBooks.com

Published 2006 by
HERITAGE BOOKS, INC.
Publishing Division
65 East Main Street
Westminster, Maryland 21157-5026

Copyright ' 2006 Barbara Palmer, Ph.D.

Other books by the author:
The Civil War Veterans of San Diego

All rights reserved. No part of this book may be reproduced or transmitted in any form or by any means, electronic or mechanical, including photocopying, recording or by any information storage and retrieval system without written permission from the author, except for the inclusion of brief quotations in a review.

International Standard Book Number: 978-0-7884-4115-9

TABLE OF CONTENTS

Introduction	1
Pedigree Chart	2
Talk to Relatives	2
Books on San Diego History	3
Prominent Figures in San Diego History	5
Indian Research	5
Early Hispanic Soldiers and Settlers	7
Family Clusters and Old Town Founders	11
American and European Settlers	15
Later Immigrant Groups	20
Theses about Prominent People	22
Additional Pedigree Charts	22
House Histories/Historical Site Board Reports	23
Family History Research Locations in San Diego	25
San Diego Historical Society	25
San Diego Public Library	26
San Diego Family History Center	27
San Diego Genealogical Society	28
Public Records	29
Office of the County Historian	30
San Diego County Public Law Library	30
The Congress of History of San Diego	30
Catholic Archives	30
Upcoming Genealogy Events	31

Specific Genealogical Records Available	31
Baptisms/Birth Records	31
Naturalization Records	32
Military Records	33
Marriage Records	35
Divorce Records	38
Occupational Records	38
Census Records	39
Voter Registers	39
City Directories	40
Newspapers	40
Church Registers	41
Property Records	41
Tax Records	42
Civil and Criminal Records	43
Hospital Records	44
Death/Burial Records	44
Probate Records/Wills	47
Coroner Records	48
Mortuary Records	48
Cemetery Records	49
Presidio/Mission San Diego Cemeteries	49
El Campo Santo at Old Town	51
San Pasqual Cemetery at Old Town	51
Protestant Cemetery at La Playa	51

Protestant Cemetery at Old Town	54
Old Jewish Cemetery	59
Calvary/Mission Hills Cemetery	60
Mount Hope Cemetery	61
Cypress View Mausoleum	62
Greenwood Memorial Park	62
Holy Cross Catholic Cemetery	63
Home of Peace Jewish Cemetery	63
Fort Rosecrans National Cemetery	64
Other Cemeteries in or near San Diego	64
Glenn Abbey Cemetery	64
La Vista Memorial Park	64
El Cajon Cemetery	65
El Camino Memorial Park	65
Books Containing Cemetery Information	65
Taking Your Research Past San Diego	67
San Diego Family History Center	67
Carlsbad Library	68
San Diego Public Library--Genealogy Room	68
Local University Libraries	69
The National Archives at Laguna Niguel	69
Conclusion	70
Index to Historical Names	71
Citations and Image Sources	81
Map of San Diego (1873) and Some Cemetery Maps	85

FAMILY HISTORY RESEARCH IN SAN DIEGO, CALIFORNIA

INTRODUCTION

While doing research at various archives around San Diego, I often overhear people say they are just beginning to do family history research, and ask librarians about what sources are available for that purpose. There are many, many research sources available locally, and to facilitate the research process, I have compiled some of the major sources into this book. This book presents a list of libraries, archives, historical societies or government entities that have records, books, photos, manuscripts, or other items of genealogical interest in San Diego, California.

But first, imagine that you are tracing an individual who lived in San Diego in 1900. Realize that your ancestor probably had the same experiences in life that you have had. They were born at XYZ location, and a birth certificate would indicate this fact. There may be records available from the hospital where they were born, and church records of their christening or baptism.

When you were growing up, you became familiar with the boundaries of the neighborhood that you lived in, and could probably locate where your neighborhood was on a map. Consult books at the library about the neighborhood where your ancestor lived.

Maps are important to family history research for they help pinpoint exactly where your ancestor's house was located and in what part of town. You might obtain an early map from the San Diego Historical Society or the California Room of the downtown San Diego Public Library which would show how developed your ancestor's neighborhood was during the time period he or she lived there.

Your ancestor went to school, so recall your own school experience. There were report cards, photos of school events, year books, and school newspapers which chronicled events at the school. I will not discuss school sources further, but if your ancestor attended a local school, visit it if it is still open. Ask to see records, scrap books, year books, and newspaper articles which might contain information about and photos of your ancestor. Also, research the school at the San Diego Historical Society or at the California Room, or read about the school in a community history.

If you are searching for a male ancestor, it is likely that he would have been in the military. I will not go into this category for recent military personnel, but there are ways to trace their records. If your ancestor served in the Civil War, there are references in this book about how to obtain more information about their unit and dates of service, their pension record, Grand Army of the Republic membership, and so on.

Your ancestor was married and perhaps also divorced. If the marriage or divorce occurred in San Diego County, public records were made of these events, which are discussed in more detail below. Your ancestor also worked and perhaps attended church in San Diego. Your knowledge of their occupation and religious affiliation will help you to uncover additional information about them from their job sites or neighborhood churches.

If your ancestor lived in San Diego from 1850 to 1930, they will appear on local census returns, which are available for research purposes only up through 1930 for privacy reasons (Note: the 1890 census was destroyed by fire and is thus not available). Printed and/or microfilmed census indexes and schedules are available at the San Diego Historical Society, the Family History Center, and the California Room of the downtown San Diego Public Library, and the San Diego Genealogical Society has printed census returns available for sale for 1850, 1852, 1860 and 1870 for a small charge. For research at other locations, the Family History Center has microfilm copies of all census returns for all census years and all states.

Your ancestor will probably appear in city directories, and these are available from the 1800s to around 1980 at the California Room of the public library and from the San Diego Historical Society.

If your ancestor purchased property, these records are at the county. A Grantor Index was transcribed by the San Diego Genealogical Society for the years 1850 to 1875, and this was a good thing, for the early property records on microfilm at the county are practically illegible. Early tax records are also available from 1850-1852 and from 1853-1863, and were transcribed by the same organization.

If your ancestor was involved in a lawsuit or in a criminal case, if he was naturalized, or if he appeared in voter registers, records of these events are available. Early church records were also transcribed by the San Diego Genealogical Society.

Your ancestor may have been the subject of an oral history interview, and these are available at the San Diego Historical Society, the California Room of the downtown San Diego Public Library, and local historical societies. I will not discuss diaries further, but if they exist, they would be at these locations.

If your ancestors donated photos, they would most likely be in the photo archives of the San Diego Historical Society, at local historical societies, or in the vertical files in the California Room of the downtown public library. Photos often accompany obituaries, and newspapers also have individual and group photos and photos of members of organizations. These would be available at the same locations.

Finally, your ancestor died and was buried. If they died in San Diego, there are a wealth of local death, probate, coroner, mortuary, and cemetery records which will be discussed in full below.

PEDIGREE CHART
Before beginning the research process, however, it would be a good idea to follow two steps. The first step is to fill out a pedigree chart. Pedigree charts can be obtained from genealogical libraries or from books on genealogy. When you fill out details about yourself and your parents, grandparents and great grandparents on a pedigree chart, the chart then provides a road map because it tells you what you know about your ancestors and what you need to find out.

Above all, family history research is a study of people and locations. If you don't know the names of your great grandparents and where they lived, for example, you will have a hard time researching them or of finding the records necessary to continue your research back to earlier generations.

On the pedigree chart, you will see that there are lines for individual names. The best of all possible worlds is to have the chart filled out for each person with at least the following information available for them: their full name, date and place of birth, date and place of marriage, and date and place of death.

If you can fill out these details for each individual on a pedigree chart, you have come a long way toward starting your family history research. The information you cannot fill out becomes the information that you must discover through additional research.

TALK TO RELATIVES
The second step is to talk to relatives to answer questions raised by your pedigree chart. Contact any relatives that have information about your family. If there is a particular relative who has kept the family papers, tape record an interview with them to get information which might never be available to you again once they pass on or leave the area. I cannot stress how important this step is, for valuable family

information is lost forever with the passing of key people.

I will not get into the topic of adoption in this book, as it is a complicated one and depends upon the availability of records and state laws in local areas. Suffice to say, adoptees are finding their families all the time, if necessary using search services to do so. Adoptees also join organizations like the Adoptees Liberty Movement Association (ALMA), which is dedicated to helping adoptees conduct their search. Locating birth families is not as impossible a task as it once was, and there is a good chance that adoptees will be able to locate their families, if they desire to do so.

After you have constructed your pedigree chart, talked with relatives, and filled out those portions of the pedigree chart that you had questions about, the next step is to continue your research using other sources. This book, for the most part, is limited to research in San Diego, but at the end of the book, I point out sources which will help you to conduct research in other locations.

BOOKS ON SAN DIEGO HISTORY

When researching families in San Diego, it is a good idea to learn a little about the history of this location. For a good overall text, consult William Smythe's *History of San Diego*, which contains a discussion of the settlement of San Diego from the earliest times to the beginning of the 20th Century. The book also has a chapter on early Hispanic historical figures and a chapter on early American settlers in San Diego. Copies of this book are available at San Diego Public Library and at the San Diego Historical Society.

For a wonderful discussion about the various historical periods of San Diego history, read a series of books by Richard Pourade which are available at the San Diego Historical Society and the San Diego Public Library and many of its branches. The titles of the books in this series, along with the historic periods that they cover, include the following (dates are approximate):

Title	Time Period Covered
The Explorers	1542-1776, early settlement
Time of the Bells	1777-1834, the Mission and Presidio periods
The Silver Dons	1835-1868, missions secularized, ranchos, Old Town
The Glory Years	1869-1898, Alonzo Horton, New San Diego, boom and bust
Gold in the Sun	1900-1919, early 20th century development
The Rising Tide	1920-1941, Navy expansion, Lindbergh Field, development of Presidio Park
City of the Dream	1942-1970, growth, freeways, Mission Valley, Mission Bay

If you are interested in information on the Rancho period of San Diego history, read Cecil Moyer's *Historic Ranchos and Adobes of San Diego*, available at the San Diego Public Library and its branches and the San Diego Historical Society.

The best book on the development of downtown or "New San Diego" as it was originally called, is Elizabeth MacPhail's *The Story of New San Diego and of its Founder Alonzo E. Horton*. The book covers the approximate years of 1850-1920, and discusses the development of an area which competed for prominence with Old Town and eventually won out. Copies of this book are available in the California Room and in the History Department at San Diego Public Library downtown and are also in the archives and for sale at the San Diego Historical Society. See also Ed Scott's *San Diego County Soldier-Pioneers 1846-1866* for a discussion of the "New Town" of a somewhat earlier era, available at the same locations.

The *Journal of San Diego History*, a publication of the San Diego Historical Society, has many articles of interest on people, communities and events in San Diego. For example, an article written by Dr. Iris Engstrand and the late county historian Mary Ward appears in Volume XX (January 1974). It discusses Rancho Guajome, the home of historic figure Cave Johnson Couts. Another example is Volume XXXVI, (Spring/Summer 1990) of the *Journal of San Diego History*, which was dedicated to the Marston House.

Included in this volume is a short history of the Marston and Gunn families.

For a good overview of Old Town and the location of historic sites and people there, read Orion Zink's "Places and People in Old Town," *Journal of San Diego History*, Volume XV (Winter 1969). In this volume, Zink reports information from interviews with several early residents of Old Town who knew the location of homes and the people who lived in them. Photos and a map are also provided to show where the earliest Old Town buildings were located. Families discussed in some detail in this volume are the Bandini, Estudillo, Machado-Silvas, and Machado-Stewart families.

The San Diego Historical Society has many early and recent *Journal of San Diego History* volumes available for sale at their book store in Balboa Park and at the Serra Museum on Presidio Hill, and the Historical Society is now providing full text of *Journal of San Diego History* articles on their website. You can also find *Journal of San Diego History* volumes at the California Room of the downtown public library, and early volumes are available at the San Diego Genealogical Society library at El Cajon. They are also available for sale at Wahrenbrocks Books and at other used bookstores around town.

There are city and county histories which contain biographies of individuals, and other books which discuss pioneers of communities like Spring Valley and El Cajon. A list of some of these books is included below, but it is by no means exhaustive. Check with libraries and historical societies at the location you are researching for additional books that might be available. City and county histories located at the public library downtown and/or at San Diego Historical Society include:

    Black, Samuel F., *San Diego County, California: A Record of Settlement, Organization, Progress and Achievement*, two volumes.

    Leberthon & Taylor, pub., *The City and County of San Diego, Illustrated*.

    Heilbron, Carl H., *History of San Diego County*.

    Lewis Publishing Company, *Illustrated History of Southern California*.

    McGrew, Clarence, *City of San Diego and San Diego County*, two volumes.

There are also books on other topics. <u>All of the books listed below are available at the public library downtown (except the Stanford book)</u> and at other locations mentioned below:

    Adema, Thomas Joseph, *Our Hills and Valleys: A History of the Helix-Spring Valley Region*. Also available at the San Diego Historical Society.

    City of Chula Vista, *Chula Vista Heritage, 1911-1986*.

    Lay, Eldonna P., *Valley of Opportunity: The History of El Cajon*.

    MacPhail, Elizabeth Reinbold, *The Influence of German Immigrants on the Growth of San Diego*. Also available at the Family History Center and San Diego Genealogical Society library.

    Palmer, Barbara, *The Civil War Veterans of San Diego*. Also available at San Diego Historical Society, the Family History Center, San Diego Genealogical Society library.

    Parker, Nathan C., *Personal Name Index to the 1856 City Directories of California*.

San Diego Historical Society, *San Diego County Pioneer Families*. Available at the San Diego Historical Society.

Scott, Ed, *San Diego County Soldier-Pioneers: 1846-1866*. Also available at the Family History Center.

Stanford, Leland Ghent, *San Diego's LLB: Legal Lore and the Bar*. Available at the Family History Center.

Wohlers, Bertha Palmer, *Follow the Light: The Palmer Family and the Savoy Theater*.

PROMINENT FIGURES IN SAN DIEGO HISTORY

Some of you will descend from individuals who are well known in San Diego history. There are books about these individuals at the San Diego Public Library, the San Diego Historical Society, and local historical societies and libraries, so visit these libraries to check their catalogs or search their catalogs online.

Many San Diego historical figures are also mentioned in Hubert Howe Bancroft's "Pioneer Register and Index" which is found in various volumes of Bancroft's *History of California*. This is an alphabetical index which runs from Volume 2 through Volume 5 of the Bancroft books as follows:

Volume 2: Names beginning with A through E
Volume 3: Names beginning with F through H
Volume 4: Names beginning with I through Q
Volume 5: Names beginning with R through Z

Listings in the Bancroft Pioneer Register and Index usually have a year stated at the beginning of a persons biographical sketch, signifying the year the pioneer arrived in California. Then follows a brief or extended biography of the person. The Pioneer Register and Index lists names from the earliest settlement of California through the mid-1850s and beyond.

Page citations in the Pioneer Register and Index may lead to comments about a pioneer in the various volumes. Regarding the time periods covered in Bancroft's volumes, Volume 1 covers the earliest years of California settlement from 1769 through 1800. Volume 2 covers 1801-1824; Volume 3 covers 1825-1840, Volume 4 covers 1840-1845, and Volume 5 covers 1846-1848 (the Mexican War era), and the Bancroft volumes continue on after that. These volumes are located at the San Diego Historical Society and at the public library downtown. Some of the volumes can also be found at various branch libraries of the public library system and at the libraries of local universities.

The following is a brief discussion of research on historical figures in San Diego, but does not by any means begin to describe all of the sources available for the study of local historical figures.

Indian Research

There are a number of sources which give information about Indians indigenous to the San Diego region. One of the best is a book by Phillip White entitled *Bibliography of the Indians of San Diego County*, which summarizes the many, many newspaper articles, books, theses and other works that have been published about local Indian groups.

The late Florence Shipek, a well known authority on local Indians, published a book entitled *Pushed Into the Rocks*, which provides an overview of local Indian history, their placement on reservations, and legislation passed to regulate local Indian tribes. Florence Shipek also wrote a book entitled *Delfina Cuero*, which presents information Shipek gathered from interviews with an Indian woman who lived in

Mission Valley and other locations after 1900. There is also an oral history interview of Florence Shipek at the San Diego Historical Society archives.

A article entitled "Cosoy, First Spanish Stop in Alta California," by Dr. Paul Ezell and Greta Ezell, is featured in *Brand Book Number Eight: San Diego Corral of the Westerners*. The article discusses the Ezell's theory of where this early Indian village was located. Also, read general histories about early San Diego such as Fr. Zephyrin Engelhardt's *Missions and Missionaries of California, Vol. 1* and Richard Pourade's book *The Explorers*, covering the 1542-1776 time period.

Richard Carrico, in his book *Strangers in a Stolen Land*, gives an overview of the Indian experience in San Diego County from about 1850 to 1880. The book is based on his University of San Diego thesis, entitled "Creation of a Marginal People, Native Americans in American San Diego, 1850-1880." A copy of Richard Carrico's thesis is available at the Copley Library of the University of San Diego.

Susan Hunter Carrico's University of San Diego thesis, entitled "Urban Indians in San Diego, 1850-1900," is featured in a book entitled *The Impact of European Exploration and Settlement on Local Native Americans*, published by the Cabrillo Historical Association in 1986. Susan Carrico's theses and the Cabrillo Historical Association's book are available at the Copley Library of the University of San Diego.

The Indian experience is explored in various articles presented in the *Journal of San Diego History* (hereafter "JSDH"), including an article on the location of the Indian village of Temecula, JSDH Vol. XVIII, No. 3 (July 1972); an article on Lovell's report on the Cahuilla Indians, JSDH Vol. XXII, No. 1 (January 1976); an article on San Diego Indians 1850-1865, JSDH Vol. XXVI, No. 3 (July 1980); and an article on Tom Lucas of Laguna Ranch, JSDH Vol. XXIX, No. 2 (April 1983).

There is also an article on the Campo Indian Agency, JSDH Vol. XXIX, No. 3 (July 1983); an article on the trial and execution of Indian Joe, JSDH Vol. XXXIII, No. 4 (October 1987); an article on Indian murderers 1850-1900, JSDH Vol. XXXVI, No. 1 (January 1990); and an article on Captain Jose Panto and the San Pascual Indian Pueblo 1835-1878, JSDH Vol. 43, No. 2 (Spring 1997).

See also articles on Catholic history such as the struggle over secularization of the Missions, JSDH Vol. XV, No. 4 (October 1969); an article on Indian labor at the California Missions, JSDH Vol XXIV, No. 2 (March 1978); and an article on St. Anthony Indian School, 1886-1907, JSDH Vol. XXXIV, No. 3, (July 1988).

Several theses listed in "Preliminary Checklist of Master's Theses and Doctoral Dissertations on the History of San Diego," JSDH Vol. 39, No. 3 (Summer 1993) also discuss the local Indian experience. Nearly all of these theses are located at San Diego State University, including a thesis entitled "Multiple World View of a Diegueno Community," by Ruth Almstedt; and "Changing Play Patterns Among Kumeyaay Diegueno Indians," by Myrna DeSomber.

Other theses at San Diego State include "An Analysis of Diegueno Pictographs," by Kenneth Hedges; "The Blessings of Bureaucracy: Indian Education in San Diego County, 1848-1947," by Nancy Miller; "The Yuman Indians of Southern California: An Interdisciplinary Synthesis," by James Moriarty. See also, "An Ethnoarcheological Approach to the Study of Acculturation Among the Cupeno Indians on the Pala Reservation," by Wendy Spear; "The Life History of a Luiseno Indian: James Martinez," by Robin Talley; and "Legends of the Diegueno Indians," by Marjorie Wilson.

A wonderful compilation of early Indian vital records is included in the R. Clinton Griffin books at the San Diego Historical Society (SDHS) or at the downtown San Diego Public Library (SDPL). Mr. Griffin indicates that these records are by no means complete and he is in the process of adding additional information to them as it becomes available to him. Of particular interest are the following books:

Mission San Diego de Alcala Baptisms, 1769-1799 (at SDHS)
Mission San Diego de Alcala Baptisms For the Mission and Vicinity: 1769-1850 (at SDPL)
Mission Basilica San Diego de Alcala: Burials for Mission and Presidio 1775-1831 (at SDHS)
El Campo Santo Cemetery [The Holy Field] San Diego, California: Burials 1849-1880 (at SDHS)

These volumes contain the names of Indians either baptized or buried at three locations--Mission San Diego de Alcala in Mission Valley, Presidio Hill adjacent to Old Town San Diego, and El Campo Santo in Old Town San Diego, although at times the baptism book appears to include baptisms in outlying areas of San Diego County as well. There are gaps in the burial records for Mission and Presidio which suggest that there may have been another burial book being kept in the early days which is no longer available.

An example of one of the most complete entries in these books is a baptism which appears to contain the full names of the parents and of an Indian child being baptized, as follows:

"On the 18th day of February 1776, Fr. Vincente Fuster baptized a day old child. Legitimate child of Joseph Maria and Mariana Rivera, both Indians of this mission. Given the name Simon Maria Rivera. Godfather Ignacio, husband of Maria Concepcion, both Indians. Signed by Fr. Fermin Francisco de Lasuen."[1]

Baptismal entries more often read like the following, however:

"On the 9th day of June 1776, a child 18 days old. Child of Indians from the rancheria San Francisco. Given the name Antonio. Godfather Juan de Ortega, Leather Jacket Soldier. Signed by Fr. Vincente Fuster."[2]

Burial information is even more abbreviated. An Indian burial from the Mission/Presidio book reads as follows: "Manuel Mariano. Buried 26 October 1776 in the Presidio cemetery. Infant. Amerindian,"[3] and a burial from the El Campo Santo book reads: "Isidora. Buried 10 June 1854. Age: 30 years. Married. Indian."[4] Consult census returns for 1850, 1852, 1860, 1870 and thereafter for names of Indian inhabitants of San Diego County, but note that the earlier census returns for Indians often give first names only.

Early Hispanic Soldiers and Settlers
The history of San Diego consists of four distinct time periods:

The Presidio Hill (1769-1821) and Mission San Diego de Alcala (1774-1846) eras: Hispanic soldiers lived on Presidio Hill near Old Town San Diego from 1769 to 1821; their families and settlers began arriving there by 1774. Franciscan missionaries occupied Mission San Diego de Alcala in Mission Valley from 1774 until Fr. Vicente Oliva left the Mission at the start of the Mexican War in 1846. At Point Loma, a small fort (Fort Guijarros) was manned sporadically (1795-1830s) to guard against military and trade incursions, and La Playa became the traditional port.

The Old Town San Diego Mexican era (1821 to 1846): The Hispanic founders moved down from Presidio Hill to start Old Town San Diego after Mexico declared its independence from Spain. Several American and European men arrive and marry into the Hispanic founding families.

The Old Town (1846-1872) and New Town (1850-1853) American/European eras: American forces and American and European settlers arrive at San Diego in the Mexican War, and by statehood (1850) were governing San Diego. A "New Town" closer to San Diego Bay is started in 1850 which fails in 1853. These eras end when a fire destroys part of Old Town's business district in 1872.

The Alonzo E. Horton era (1867+): Alonzo Ebenezer Horton founds modern downtown San Diego adjacent to the former "New Town", and the American and European population gravitates there.

The Presidio Hill era began when Spanish soldiers and Franciscan missionaries arrived at San Diego from Mexico in 1769 to claim California for Spain and to convert the indigenous population to Christianity. The 1769 Expedition arrived in four parties, two by land and two by sea. The two sea parties aboard the *San Antonio* and the *San Carlos* which arrived on April 11 and April 28, 1769, came to California primarily to transport supplies for the soldiers and missionaries, although a group of volunteer soldiers from Cataluna, Spain, also arrived on the *San Carlos*. Nearly all of the men on the *San Carlos* became sick of or died from scurvy during the trip from Mexico, and the men on the other ship did not remain long in California.

The first of the land expeditions, led by Captain Fernando Javier de Rivera y Moncada, arrived at San Diego on May 14, 1769, and the second land expedition, led by Gaspar de Portola and Fr. Junipero Serra, arrived at San Diego on July 1, 1769. Some men from the two land expeditions and five Catalonian volunteers from the *San Carlos* remained to become founders of the earliest Hispanic families in California.

An excellent source for the history of Presidio Hill and of the land expeditions which arrived there is Harry W. Crosby's book *Gateway to Alta California* (San Diego, Sunbelt Publications, 2003). In the book, Harry Crosby discusses the experiences of the early soldiers and missionaries of the land expeditions in Lower California, and then tells what happened to them after they arrived in San Diego.

Crosby then lists individual members of the two land parties, gives brief biographies of these men and their experiences after arrival in California, and also provides details about them, where available, including their race, date and location of their birth and death, and information about their parents, wives and children. Men with biographies in *Gateway to Alta California* (underlined names indicate men who died and were buried at San Diego) included: Francisco Javier Aguilar, Bernardino de Alvarado, Juan Bautista de Alvarado, Sebastian de Alvitre, Pedro Antonio Amador, Jose Gabriel de Arce, Sebastian Constantino de Arce, Manuel Antonio Badiola, <u>Jose Maria Bejarano (Vegerano)</u> and <u>Juan Evangelista Benno</u>.

Also Jose Anastasio Camacho, Jose de Canizares, <u>Guillermo Carrillo</u>, Mariano Carrillo, Agustin Castelo, Juan Antonio Coronel, Andres de Cota, Pablo Antonio de Cota, Fr. Juan Crespi, Juan Jose Dominguez, Jose Joaquin Espinoza, Jose Maria de Gongora, <u>Alejo Antonio Gonzalez</u>, Jose Ignacio de la Higuera, "Ignacio" (a servant of Gaspar Portola), Sebastian Manriquez, Juan Maria Miranda, Francisco Javier Ochoa, Jose Gabriel de Ojeda, Jose Francisco de Ortega, Juan Ismerio de Osuna, Juan Luis de Osuna and Gaspar de Portola.

Also Martin Reyes, Fernando Javier de Rivera y Moncada, Juan Jose de Robles, Bernardo Rubio, Jose Carlos Rubio, Antonio Vicente Ruiz, Fr. Junipero Serra, Alejandro Soto (Sotomayor), Mateo Ignacio Soto, Sebastian Tarabal, Antonio Trasvina, Juan Bautista Valdes, Jose Velasquez, Mariano Verdugo, Narciso Verdugo and Anastasio Verduzco.

The men from Crosby's land expeditions with descendants who later helped to found Old Town San Diego included Mariano Carrillo and Andres de Cota of the Rivera land expedition and Jose Francisco de Ortega, Pedro Antonio Amador, Jose Gabriel de Arce and Pablo Antonio de Cota of the Portola/Serra land expedition. Juan Ismerio de Osuna, a soldier who Harry Crosby indicated had come to California "which party, unknown" would also become the ancestor of many descendants at Old Town.

Juan Jose Dominguez, who also arrived at San Diego in 1769 "which party, unknown" and never married, later bequeathed his Rancho San Pedro near Los Angeles to his nephew Cristobal Dominguez, who with his wife Maria Reyes-Ybanez owned one of the first houses in Old Town San Diego. Their daughter, Maria Victoria, married Jose Antonio Estudillo and they owned the Estudillo house, the finest house in Old Town.

One man not mentioned in Harry Crosby's book was Antonio Yorba, a Catalonian volunteer who arrived on the *San Carlos*, one of the ships of the 1769 Expedition. Yorba, who was on Presidio Hill in 1769 and from 1789 to about 1810 also had descendants who helped to found Old Town. In fact, Yorba had eleven children born at San Diego from 1789 to 1810 plus five children who were born at Monterey prior to 1789, three from his first wife. Antonio Yorba died and was buried at Mission San Juan Capistrano in 1825.

Another man not mentioned in Harry Crosby's book was Joseph Raymundo Carrillo, who was identified by Marie E. Northrop in her *Spanish-Mexican Families of Early California: 1769-1850* as having arrived in California on the Portola/Serra land expedition. Two of Carrillo's seven children were born on Presidio Hill in 1791 and 1794, and Carrillo was buried on Presidio Hill on November 10, 1808. Northrop also indicates that Joseph Maria Soberanes arrived on the Portola/Serra Expedition, although Soberanes does not appear to have had any descendants who helped to found Old Town San Diego.

Another author who wrote about the Presidio Hill era was the late William M. Mason, a former Curator of Southern California History at the Los Angeles County Museum of Natural History. Mason was the author of "The Garrisons of San Diego Presidio: 1770-1794", *Journal of San Diego History*, Vol. XXIV, No. 4, (Fall 1978), pp. 399-424, which provided garrison lists of soldiers on Presidio Hill just after the time period studied by Harry Crosby in *Gateway to Alta California*. The garrison lists detailed which soldiers were on Presidio Hill and when they were there. This article can be accessed on the Internet at the San Diego Historical Society website by clicking on "Journals" and searching for William Mason or this article.

On the garrison list for May 20, 1782 ("Garrisons", pp. 412-413), the soldiers are named and other details are given for those with the rank of corporal or below, including their age, birthplace, marital status, race and literacy. The article also includes the 1790 census for San Diego ("Garrisons", pp. 415-419), naming the soldiers and settlers on Presidio Hill along with their wives and children. This list includes information about military rank, race, birthplace, age, marital status, and nativity of all enumerated, where available.

In addition to the men of the 1769 Expedition with descendants who later helped to found Old Town San Diego (Amador, Arce, Cota, Carrillo, Dominguez, Ortega, Osuna and Yorba), the following soldiers or settlers on the Mason lists also had descendants who helped to found Old Town: Pablo de Grijalva, Juan Antonio Ibarra (Ybarra), Pedro Lisalde, Juan Francisco Lopez, Manuel Nieto, Santiago de la Cruz Pico, his son Jose Maria Pico, Feliciano Rios, Felipe Romero, Mateo Rubio, Ignacio Ruiz, Francisco Xavier Sepulveda, Francisco Serrano, Jose Miguel Silvas, his son Joseph Manuel Silvas, and Ignacio Soto.

William Mason is also author of *The Census of 1790* (Novato, CA: Ballena Press, 1998) which gives a better idea of who was in California by 1781. Mason first provides a list compiled by Fernando Javier de Rivera y Moncada of soldiers and several of their wives who were in California on January 1, 1775. He then lists soldiers, colonists, wives and children who arrived on the Anza Expedition of 1775-1776 and on the Rivera Expedition of 1781, after which he recites the 1790 census for the entire state of California for the only communities then in existence on the California frontier. These settlements included the following, along with the approximate number of married couples or single individuals who lived there in 1790:

San Diego (pp. 77-82)	37 married couples	20 single men
Los Angeles (pp. 82-86)	22 married couples	9 singles (4 widows, 1 widower, 4 single men)
Santa Barbara (pp. 86-92)	43 married couples	25 singles (1 widow, 5 widowers, 19 single men)
Monterey (pp. 92-98)	40 married couples	34 singles (3 widows, 2 widowers, 29 single men)
San Jose (pp. 98-100)	15 married couples	3 singles (1 widower, 2 single men)
San Francisco (pp. 100-104)	28 married couples	13 singles (1 widower, 12 single men)

The following missions were also founded in the early years of settlement:

Mission San Diego de Alcala at San Diego, founded on July 16, 1769
Mission San Carlos Borromeo near Carmel, founded on June 3, 1770
Mission San Antonio de Padua, 20 miles from King City, founded on July 14, 1771
Mission San Gabriel Archangel at San Gabriel, founded on September 8, 1771

Mission San Luis Obispo de Tolosa at San Luis Obispo, founded on September 1, 1772
Mission San Francisco de Asis (Mission Dolores) at San Francisco, founded on June 29, 1776
Mission San Juan Capistrano at San Juan Capistrano, founded on November 1, 1776
Mission Santa Clara de Asis at Santa Clara, founded on January 12, 1777
Mission San Buenaventura at Ventura, 60 miles north of Los Angeles, founded on March 31, 1782
Mission Santa Barbara at Santa Barbara, founded on December 16, 1786
Mission La Purisima Conception, five miles north of Lompoc, founded on December 8, 1787

These were the only population centers in California by 1790, and as noted the population at each location was very small. In *The Census of 1790*, families and individuals were enumerated at the major settlements but only the mayordomos (foremen) and their families were enumerated at the missions. To give an idea of the number of children couples were having at a particular location, of the married couples with children at San Diego in 1790, six couples had one child; six couples had two children; four couples had three children; seven couples had four children; and seven couples had five children.

Regarding the birthplaces of adults on the 1790 census, Mason indicates that they were primarily from the following locations: Villa Sinaloa (115); Loreto (45); Alamos (35), Culiacan (18), Rosario (16), Cosala (12), El Fuerte (11), Guadalajara (10), Horcasitas (10), Terrenate (10), Tepic (9), Yaqui River (8), Altar (8), Mexico City (7), San Xavier de Cabazan (6), San Bartolome (6) and "Sonora" (5). The remaining locations provided only four or fewer adults on the 1790 census (including one from Belgium and one from Cuba).

As to the later settlement of California, Mason continues in *The Census of 1790* that because of fear of English invasion, 75 Catalonian Volunteers and about 20 artillerymen arrived in 1796, but nearly all of these men were withdrawn in 1803 and 1804. A score of convicts sent to help colonize California arrived between 1797 and 1800, but not all of them remained after their time was served. Seven or eight families were sent in 1797 to populate Branciforte, now a part of Santa Cruz.

Additionally, 10 boys and 10 girls came in 1800 from an orphanage in Puebla who all shared the common surname of Lorenzana, the surname of the Bishop of Puebla (although one boy died enroute), and most of these children remained in California. Two detachments of 100 soldiers each arrived in 1819 to repel attacks of privateer Hypoloyte Bouchard, who had seized Monterey in 1818. About half of the detachment from the old Presidio at Mazatlan, which was divided between the Presidios of Santa Barbara and San Diego, remained in California, while less than half from San Blas stayed at San Francisco and Monterey.

William Mason continues, in *The Census of 1790*: "By 1790, then, most of the colonial Californians had arrived. ... By 1790 the population of California's colonials was about 1,000; in 1794, it had increased to about 1,250. In 1800, thanks to the Catalonians, artillerymen, convicts, et al., the population had increased to 1,790. This would represent an average increase of about 90 per year, as opposed to about 50 per year between 1790 and 1794. But by 1808, four years after the withdrawal of the new units had taken place, there were only 1,950, which is an average increase of only about 20 per year. Most of the growth, by far, was from natural increase between 1790 and 1820.

"More telling evidence comes from an examination of various population lists of California communities between 1821 and 1830. In canvassing the adults in these lists 30 or 40 years after 1790, we discover the majority are descended from people who were already in California in 1790. The percentages are impressive: a census for Monterey in 1827--84% [descended from those who were in California in 1790]. For San Jose in 1830--88%; San Diego's garrison list for 1821--71%. Over half of the new people on San Diego's list were from Baja California. San Francisco's garrison list in 1829--82%... Santa Barbara's Easter census in 1825--84%. ... Los Angeles' Easter census for 1823--78%...

"It would be safe to say that about 80% or more of California's non-Indian population, the *gente de razon*, were descended from colonists who had come prior to 1790. ... It is quite unlikely that more than 300 people settled permanently in California between 1790 and 1820, if that many." Mason, *The Census of 1790*, pp. 40-41, 44.[5] Mason adds: "Even as late as 1846, the pioneers who had arrived before 1790 and their descendants were still in the majority. Even taking into consideration the filtration into California between 1790 and 1819, those who had come earlier were the backbone of the province at the end of the Mexican regime. (Mason, *The Census of 1790*), p. 114.)[6]

Another indispensable source of genealogical information for early Hispanic families is a set of books in two volumes by Marie Northrop entitled *Spanish-Mexican Families of Early California: 1769-1850*, mentioned above. These books are available at the California Room of the San Diego Public Library, the San Diego Historical Society, the Family History Center and the San Diego Genealogical Society library.

The Northrop books can be purchased from Southern California Genealogical Society, 417 Irving Drive, Burbank, CA 91504-2408; phone (818) 843-7247; fax (818) 843-7262. The Southern California Genealogical Society was first given permission to publish Volume II of the Northrop books and later was given permission to publish Volume I. A brochure for these books states:

> Volume I was developed from Thomas Workman Temple II's 'Genealogical Tables of Spanish and Mexican Families of California.' Most of the colonists came from Northwest Mexico between 1769 and 1781 and numbered between 600 and 700 persons. The population increase to about 3,000 over the next 40 years resulted more from a healthy birthrate than from immigration. This second edition, extensively revised and expanded, was reprinted in 1999.
>
> Volume II lists 265 family groups outside of Temple's Genealogical Tables in a format similar to Volume I. Included are the 11 founding families of the Pueblo of Los Angeles and 46 of the soldiers and their families who accompanied them on the overland expedition from Sonora and Sinaloa in northern Mexico. Volume II was reprinted in 1999.

The Northrop books give listings for the families discussed in the books and show, if available, where the parents and children were born or baptized, where they married, and where they died or were buried. In some instances, two or three generations of a family are included in these volumes, and one can trace the migration of the families in California by noting where the children of the families were born.

Because the Northrop books list families, no single soldiers or settlers appear to be included in these volumes unless they were widows or widowers, but single individuals can be discovered in the 1790 census for California. A third volume of the Northrop books is now available from Southern California Genealogical Society as of mid-2005.

Family Clusters and Old Town Founders
A clustering of family groups probably occurred on Presidio Hill and the clustering in some instances became more evident when some of the families later moved down to Old Town. One early cluster of families on Presidio Hill was the Carrillo/Ortega/Verdugo/Ruiz cluster. This cluster first consisted of brothers Joseph Raymundo Carrillo, Guillermo Carrillo and Mariano Carrillo and their sister Maria Antonia Victoria Carrillo, wife of Jose Francisco de Ortega, plus any children born to Joseph Raymundo Carrillo and to the Ortegas (Guillermo and Mariano Carrillo remained single).

Soldiers Jose Maria, Juan Maria, Mariano and Ygnacio Leonardo Verdugo (sons of Maria Ygnacia Carrillo, a sister of the early Carrillos and wife of Juan Diego Verdugo) would have been members of this cluster as would bachelor soldier Francisco Maria Ruiz (whose mother or grandmother may have been Isabel Carrillo, a sister of the early Carrillos and wife of Juan Maria Ruiz). Joaquin Carrillo, who arrived at Presidio Hill by 1809, was a probable nephew of these Carrillos and would also have been in this cluster.

While descendants of Joseph Raymundo Carrillo and the Verdugos did not seem to play a part in the founding of Old Town San Diego, Joaquin Carrillo and Francisco Maria Ruiz both lived on Presidio Hill, where Ruiz was one of the last Commandants, and both later lived at Old Town. Ruiz built the first house and garden in Old Town, and he later granted his house to the family of Joaquin Carrillo.

There would no doubt have been a family cluster around widower Vicente Feliz and his children. This family later migrated to the Los Angeles area where Feliz was granted Los Feliz Rancho which is now the Griffith Park area of Los Angeles. For a time, Vicente Feliz was *comisionado* of the Los Angeles Pueblo, a position which was "something of an Indian agent, military attache, police chief, militia head and city manager," according to William Mason, "The Garrisons...," p. 420.[7]

There was a family cluster around Santiago de la Cruz Pico, who served as a soldier on Presidio Hill as did his son Jose Maria Pico. Jose Maria Pico's son Pio Pico, who spent his early years on Presidio Hill and in Old Town, was the last Mexican governor of California and granted large ranchos to his friends before leaving office when the Mexican War began. Pio Pico in his *Historical Narrative* discusses his early life in San Diego, and this book is available at the downtown San Diego Public Library. Pio Pico's brother, Andres Pico, was one of the signers of the Treaty of Guadalupe Hidalgo at the end of the Mexican War.

Soldiers from Presidio Hill also married several Cota sisters, daughters of Roque Jacinto de Cota, who lived for a while on Presidio Hill but later resided at Mission San Gabriel. The following siblings also lived on Presidio Hill at various times: Maria Lucinda Rodriguez, Juana Maria Simona Rodriguez and Vicente Villa Rodriguez; Ana Maria Gertrudis Silvas, Maria Bernarda Silvas, Maria Josefa Gabriela Silvas, Maria Balbaneda Silvas and Joseph Manuel Silvas; and Juan Crispin Perez Nieto and Jose Manuel Perez Nieto.

An important family cluster prior to 1806, when the Machado family can be placed on Presidio Hill by the birth date of their first child, was a grouping of the Lopez and allied families. These families clustered around the founding ancestors Juan Francisco Lopez and his wife Maria Feliciana Arballo, the widow of Josef Gutierrez. As Marie Northrop indicates in *Spanish-Mexican Families of Early California*, Vol. 1, pp. 200-202, Juan Francisco Lopez and Maria Feliciana Arballo had children who were born in San Diego in 1778, 1789, 1791 and 1793 and children born at San Juan Capistrano in 1781, 1782, 1784 and 1786.

The Lopez family cluster included Maria Eustaquia Gutierrez and Maria Thomasa Gutierrez, daughters of Maria Feliciana Arballo and Josef Gutierrez. The Lopez family cluster merged with the Aguilar, Alvarado, Alvarez, Amador, Arce, Carrillo, Cota, Marron, Morillo, Ortega, Osuna, Pena, Pico, Rosas, Silvas, Villalobo and Yorba families to form some of the most important family alliances at Presidio Hill and Old Town.

The families who lived longest on Presidio Hill were the families of Maximo Alanis, Pedro Alvarez, Joseph Raymundo Carrillo, Cristobal Dominguez, Jose Antonio Ruiz Leiva (whose widow Clara Sinusin later married Manuel Bustamante) and the families of Juan Antonio Ibarra (Ybarra), Pedro Antonio Lisalde, Juan Francisco Lopez, Juan Maria Olivera, Felipe Romero, Mateo Rubio, Francisco Sotelo, Juan Valenzuela, Antonio Yorba and Vicente Feliz and his children.

Several soldiers or settlers who arrived on Presidio Hill and who later played an important part in the founding of Old Town after 1821 deserve discussion, including the following:

> Francisco Maria Ruiz, mentioned above. Ruiz was on Presidio Hill in 1775 and later returned to become the acting commandant of the Presidio from 1806-1807, 1809-1820 and from September 1821 to 1827. Ruiz built several of the earliest houses at Old Town and became the owner of Rancho Penasquitos. He retired at age 73 and died after 1836.
>
> Juan Maria Osuna, the son of Juan Ismerio de Osuna of the 1769 Expedition, arrived as a soldier on Presidio Hill by 1806. Juan Maria Osuna's wife was Maria Juliana Josefa Lopez of the Lopez

family cluster, and they would own a house north of the plaza at Old Town San Diego. Juan Maria Osuna was the first *alcalde* of San Diego in 1835, a Justice of the Peace and the grantee of San Dieguito Rancho. The Osunas are buried at El Campo Santo cemetery at Old Town.

Joseph Manuel Machado, a corporal of the Presidio Hill company, arrived in San Diego with his wife Maria Serafina Valdes about 1806, according to the birth year of their first child. Their parents came with the Rivera expedition in 1781 and were residing at Santa Barbara by 1790. Machado descendants would later own several properties at Old Town San Diego and Machado daughters would marry a number of American and several European settlers (see below). Joseph Manuel Machado and Maria Serafina Valdes are buried at El Campo Santo cemetery in Old Town.

Juan Maria Marron Sr. arrived on Presidio Hill by 1806, the year he married Maria de la Luz Ruiz, the daughter of Ignacio Ruiz and Maria Gorgona Valenzuela, who were on the 1790 census for San Diego. Their son, Juan Maria Marron, Jr. would marry Maria Felipa Osuna, granddaughter of Juan Ismerio de Osuna, and they would own a house on the east side of Old Town plaza. Juan Maria Marron, Jr. and Maria Felipa Osuna are buried at El Campo Santo cemetery in Old Town.

Joaquin Carrillo, probable nephew of the earliest Carrillos on Presidio Hill, arrived as a soldier on Presidio Hill by 1809 and was living as a retired soldier at Old Town by 1827. He married Maria Ignacia Candelaria Lopez of the Lopez family cluster, and their daughter Maria Josefa Carrillo would marry Henry Delano Fitch, American settler, merchant and trader, in 1829 (see below).

Cristobal Dominguez was a soldier at Presidio Hill before 1800 and later served as sergeant of the troops until his retirement in 1821. He and his wife Maria Reyes-Ybanez owned one of the first houses in Old Town. As mentioned above, Cristobal Dominguez inherited Rancho San Pedro from his uncle Juan Jose Dominguez of the 1769 Expedition. He obtained title to the rancho around 1823 and his sons went on to develop the property after Cristobal Dominguez died and was buried on Presidio Hill in 1825. See Robert Cameron Gillingham's book *The Rancho San Pedro: The Story of a Famous Rancho in Los Angeles County and of its Owners The Dominguez Family* (San Pedro, CA: Dominguez Properties, revised ed. 1983) for more information about this family. The book is at the downtown San Diego Public Library.

Santiago Arguello arrived as a soldier on Presidio Hill by 1818 and became paymaster for the troops. He was the son of Jose Dario Arguello, a Commandant at San Francisco, Monterey and Santa Barbara and acting governor of California from 1814 to 1815. Santiago Arguello's wife was Maria del Pilar Ortega, the granddaughter of Jose Francisco de Ortega of the 1769 Expedition and his wife Maria Antonia Victoria Carrillo. Santiago Arguello was a lieutenant of the San Diego Company and then Commandant from 1830 to 1835. He was also an important leader and landowner in San Diego, and the first proprietor of Rancho Tijuana, where he died in 1862.

Jose Maria Estudillo, lieutenant of the Monterey Company from 1804 to 1827, became Commandant of the San Diego Company from 1827 until his death and burial on Presidio Hill in 1830. His wife was Gertrudis Horcasitas, and a well known son was Jose Antonio Estudillo, who married Maria Victoria Dominguez, the daughter of Cristobal Dominguez and Maria Reyes-Ybanez, and built the finest house in Old Town after being granted a house lot there in 1827.

Juan Bandini was at San Diego by 1822. His father, Jose Bandini, was born in Spain of Italian heritage, and he was on a military mission in Peru where Juan was born in 1800. On November 20, 1822, Juan Bandini married Maria Dolores Damiana Estudillo, the daughter of Jose Maria Estudillo, on Presidio Hill, and the Bandinis would also have one of the finest houses in Old Town. Bandini was a large landowner, a highly political figure and active in state politics for many years. He also had one of the finest salons in California. One Bandini daughter married Abel Stearns and another daughter married Cave Couts, two important figures in California history (see below).

Francisco Maria Alvarado arrived at Old Town probably around 1829, the year of his marriage to Maria Tomasa Pico of the Pico family cluster. Alvarado became the city treasurer in 1840-1841 and Justice of the Peace in 1845, and the Alvarados owned one of the early houses at Old Town. Francisco Maria Alvarado would come to own Rancho Penasquitos, and he and his relatives would evetually be the largest landowners in North San Diego County.

Other founders of Old Town included trader Jose Antonio Aguirre and Miguel de Pedrorena, who both came to San Diego from Spain and both married into the Estudillo family.

Soldiers and settlers from Presidio Hill began to move down to Old Town around 1821 when Mexico gained its independence from Spain. The first houses at Old Town were those of Francisco Maria Ruiz, Juan Bandini, Jose Antonio Estudillo, Pio and Andres Pico, Juan Maria Marron, Francisco Maria Alvarado, Juan Jose Rocha, Rafaela Serrano, Juan Rodriguez, Rosario Aguilar and Joseph Manuel Machado.

William Smythe, in his *History of San Diego*, pp. 161-177, presents short biographies of early Hispanic settlers at Old Town, including: Blas Aguilar, Rosario Aguilar, Jose Antonio Aguirre, Damasio Alipas, Gervasio Alipas, Jose Antonio Altamirano, Francisco Maria Alvarado, Juan Bautista Alvarado, Jose Ramon Arguello, Santiago Arguello, Santiago E. Arguello, Juan Bandini, Domingo Carrillo, Jose Antonio Carrillo, Jose Raimundo Carrillo, Joaquin Carrillo, Cristobal Dominguez, Jose Maria Echeandia, Jose Antonio Estudillo, Jose Guadalupe Estudillo and Jose Maria Estudillo.

Also Jose Antonio Gurerra y Noriega, Bonifacio Lopez, Apolinaria Lorenzana, Joseph Manuel Machado, Juan Maria Marron, Sylvester Marron, Fr. Antonio Menendez, Juan Maria Osuna, Leandro Osuna, Ramon Osuna, Miguel de Pedrorena, Andres Pico, Jose Antonio Bernardo Pico, Jose Maria Pico, Pio Pico, Juan Jose Rocha, Francisco Maria Ruiz, Jose Antonio Serrano, Fr. Antonio Ubach and Augustin V. Zamarano.

Other books about the early Hispanic founders of Presidio Hill and Old Town include Richard Pourade's *The Explorers, Time of the Bells* and *The Silver Dons*. Some of the early Spanish families were granted large land holdings and these are discussed in Cecil Moyer's *Historic Ranchos and Adobes of San Diego* and in *Some Old Ranchos and Adobes*, by Philip S. Rush. The Pourade, Moyer and Rush books are all available at the downtown San Diego Public Library, and the Pourade and Moyer books are also widely available at branch libraries throughout the San Diego Public Library system.

The Old Town Descendant's Group is an excellent source for information about the early founding families of San Diego. They have meetings on a regular basis and have a large selection of pedigree charts and books which can be researched at their meetings. Contact Old Town San Diego State Historic Park for more information about this group at (619) 220-5420.

There are also pedigree charts available for some Old Town families in *Early San Diego, CA Families: Vols. I and II*, available at the Family History Center in San Diego. Pedigree charts are available for the following families: Altamirano, Alvarado, Ames, Arguello, Connors, Cota, Couts, Dominguez, Estudillo (in Vol. I) and Lopez, Machado, Pico, Pio Pico and Serrano (in Vol. II.) Pedigree charts involving Alonzo Horton are also included in Vol. II. These volumes have been at the Family History Center for some time and probably do not contain more recent information gathered by the Old Town Descendants group. Four additional books of interest are available at the downtown San Diego Public Library:

Saddleback Ancestors: Rancho Families of Orange County, California, published by Orange County California Genealogical Society.

Ranchos Become Cities, by W.W. Robinson, discussing ranchos of Los Angeles County.

An Illustrated History of Mexican Los Angeles 1781 - 1985, by Antonio Rios-Bustamante and Pedro Castillo

Los Angeles: The End of the Rainbow, by Merry Ovnick.

Other *Journal of San Diego History* articles include: "The Political History of a Mexican Pueblo: San Diego from 1825 to 1845, Parts 1-2," JSDH Vol. XII, Nos. 3-4 (July and October 1966); "Pueblo Postscript: San Diego During the Mexican Period, 1825-1840," JSDH Vol. XIII, No. 1 (January 1967); and "Native of Arica: Requiem for a Don (Juan Bandini), JSDH Vol. XVII, No. 2 (April 1971).

See also "California's Hispanic Heritage: A View into the Spanish Myth," JSDH Vol. XIX, No. 1 (January 1973); "The Hispanic Heritage and the Borderlands," JSDH Vol. XIX, No. 3 (July 1973); and "Viva Los Californios! The Battle of San Pasqual," JSDH Vol. XIX, No. 4 (October 1973).

Later *Journal of San Diego History* articles include an article on Chicano History and an article on the true origins of Spanish officials and missionaries, both in JSDH Vol. XXIII, No. 1 (January 1977). The whole issue of the JSDH Vol. XXIV, No. 1 (January 1978) is on Spanish colonization of the Californias. There is also an article on Jose Antonio Aguirre, Spanish Merchant, in JSDH Vol. XXIX, No. 1 (January 1983); an article on the pueblo lands of San Diego, JSDH Vol. XXXVII, No. 2 (April 1991); and an article on the Mexican Catholic experience in San Diego, JSDH Vol. XXXVII, No. 4 (October 1991).

You can also visit Old Town State Park and see homes of the early Hispanic families, including those of the Estudillo, Bandini, Machado-Wrightington, Machado-Silvas, Machado-Stewart, Alvarado-Johnson, Altamirano, Aguirre and Pedrorena families. Old Town State Park is located at the intersection of Interstate 5 south at Interstate 8. The address is 4002 Wallace Street, San Diego, CA 92110.

Finally, many descendants of the early Hispanic families are buried either on Presidio Hill, at El Campo Santo cemetery in Old Town, or at Calvary Cemetery in Mission Hills, and the R. Clinton Griffin records provide burial information for these individuals (see "Burial Records" below). However, at least one famous Old Town resident is buried elsewhere. Juan Bandini and his second wife Maria del Refugio Arguello are buried at New Calvary Cemetery in Los Angeles along with his daughter Maria Arcadia Bandini, the widow of Abel Stearns, and her second husband, Col. Robert S. Baker.

American and European Settlers
American visitors began arriving at San Diego on ships in the early 1800s. One of the first of these was William Alden Gale of Boston, who came to San Diego in 1810, per Bancroft's "Pioneer Register" (other arrival dates below are from this source or from William Smythe's *History of San Diego*). Gale was a clerk aboard the ship *Albatross* in 1810, and later returned in 1822 as supercargo of the ship *Sachem*.

By 1825, Gale had returned as part owner of the *Sachem* and stayed in California for two years. He began trading for the hides and tallow of the many cattle that roamed the former mission lands, and promoted this trade to the Boston firm of Bryant & Sturgis, who entered into the trade with Californians by the mid- to late 1820s. On May 21, 1827 at Presidio Hill, Gale married Maria Francisca Marcelina Dominguez, the daughter of Cristobal Dominguez and Maria Reyes-Ybanez, and Mrs. Gale died in 1828 possibly on the voyage with her husband back to Boston. Gale later made several trips back to California, including a trip in 1829 on the Bryant & Sturgis ship *Brookline*. Along on the voyage was the *Brookline*'s clerk, a young man named Alfred Robinson, who would become one of California's pioneers.

William Alden Gale was the first American to marry into a Presidio Hill family although he did not live on Presidio Hill or at Old Town for extended periods of time. Others began arriving on Presidio Hill and later at Old Town and brief biographies for these men are as follows:

Henry Delano Fitch, the first American to marry and settle at Old Town, was born May 7, 1799 at New Bedford, Massachusetts, according to Marie Northrop's *Spanish-Mexican Families of Early California*, Vol. 2, p. 86. (Note: hereafter, citations to page numbers in the Northrop volumes where available will read like the one applicable to Fitch, i.e. N2/86, meaning that Fitch's information appears in Marie Northrop's Vol. 2 ["N2"] at page 86).

Fitch, the son of Beriah Fitch and Sally Delano and a descendant of John Howland and Richard Warren of the *Mayflower*, came to California in 1826 and eloped with Maria Josefa Carrillo, the daughter of Joaquin Carrillo, marrying her on July 3, 1829 at Mission Valparaiso, Chile.

Fitch lived out his life as a merchant at Old Town and "Died January 13, 1849 at 4 o'clock and 20 minutes in the afternoon...at the old Fitch house on Fitch or Calhoun Street ... He died of fever after a brief illness" (Henry Fitch's grave inscription, note of Judge Benjamin Hayes in 1873, from the unpublished diary, notes, letters of Judge Hayes in Cave Couts' possession--Winifred Davidson's 1932 notes, San Diego Historical Society).[8] Fitch was buried in the ruins of the chapel on Presidio Hill near the graves of daughter Natalia and Joseph Snook. Josefa Fitch and children moved to Sotoyomi Ranch near Healdsburg in Sonoma County, where she died January 26, 1893.

Abel Stearns, a native of Boston, arrived in California in 1829. He married Maria Arcadia Bandini, the daughter of Juan Bandini and his first wife Maria Dolores Damiana Estudillo, at Mission San Gabriel on June 22, 1841 (N2/23). The Stearns family moved to the Los Angeles area and Abel Stearns became the largest owner of land and cattle in Southern California. After Abel Stearns died in 1871, Arcadia Bandini Stearns married Col. Robert S. Baker of Providence, Rhode Island, on April 20, 1875 at the Los Angeles Plaza Church. The "Arcadia Block" near the Olvera Street historic district in downtown Los Angeles is named after her.

Joseph Francis Snook, a native of Weymouth, Dorset, England, was trading along the California coast by or before 1830. He married Maria Antonia Alvarado on December 2, 1837 at the "Church of the Port", presumably on Presidio Hill. She was the daughter of Juan Bautista Alvarado and Maria Raymunda Fermina Yorba and the granddaughter of Antonio Yorba of the 1769 Expedition. The Snooks owned a house north of Old Town Plaza and also owned Rancho San Bernardo (now Rancho Bernardo) in North San Diego County. Joseph Snook died on February 23, 1848 and was buried in the ruins of the old chapel nave on Presidio Hill near Henry Delano Fitch and Fitch's daughter Natalia. Maria Snook then married Henry Clayton, San Diego County's first surveyor.

John Forster, a native of England, came to California in 1833. He married Maria Isidora Ygnacia Pico ca. 1837 (N2/214). She was the granddaughter of Santiago Pico and Maria Jacinta Vastida, who arrived at Presidio Hill by 1777, and the granddaughter of Maria Feliciana Arballo and her first husband Josef Gutierrez. The Forsters eventually settled on land which is now Camp Pendleton in North San Diego County, previously owned by Pio and Andres Pico, Mrs. Forster's brothers.

Thomas Ridington (Wrightington), a native of Fall River, Massachusetts, came to San Diego in 1833 aboard the *Ayacucho*. He married Juana de Dios Machado on January 27, 1842 (N1/222), the widow of Damasio Alipas and the daughter of Joseph Manual Machado and Maria Serafina Valdes. The Wrightingtons lived in a house at the northwest corner of Old Town Plaza which is still standing. Thomas Wrightington is buried at El Campo Santo cemetery in Old Town and Juana Machado is buried at Calvary Cemetery in Mission Hills. The marriages of Machado daughters and granddaughters to American and European settlers will be discussed below.

Thomas Russell, a native of Boston, Massachusetts, came to California in 1835 and operated a hide house at La Playa. He married Maria Angeles Ibarra (Ybarra) in 1836, granddaughter of Juan Antonio Ibarra (Ybarra) and Maria de los Angeles Velasquez, who arrived at Presidio hill by 1782.

Edward Stokes, a native of England, arrived in California in 1840, and married Maria del Refugio de Jesus Ortega on June 12, 1842 (N1/249). She was the great granddaughter of Jose Francisco de Ortega of the Portola/Serra land expedition of 1769 and his wife Maria Antonia Victoria Carrillo. The Stokes family owned Pamo and Santa Ysabel Ranchos. After his death, Maria Ortega Stokes married Agustin Olvera (Olvera Street in Los Angeles is named after him).

Philip Crosthwaite, a native of Athy, County Kildare, Ireland, arrived in California in 1845, and in 1848 married Maria Josefa Lopez, the great granddaughter of Juan Francisco Lopez and Maria Feliciana Arballo. The Crosthwaites probably lived first with her father Bonifacio Lopez at Old Town, then rented the abandoned buildings at Mission San Diego de Alcala in Mission Valley, then moved to an adobe house in Mission Valley and finally settled on their ranch in Lower California. Philip Crosthwaite died at San Diego in 1903, and is buried at Mount Hope Cemetery.

Charles Robinson Johnson of Boston, the son of Beannois Johnson and Abigail Robinson, arrived in California in 1846, and on January 16, 1851 married Maria Dolores Caledonia Bandini, daughter of Juan Bandini and Maria del Refugio Arguello, in the sala of the Bandini House at Old Town (N2/24). The Johnsons lived in Los Angeles, then at the Derby-Pendleton House at Old Town and later retired to their Guadalupe Ranch in Mexico, located about 50 miles southeast of San Diego.

John F. Brown, a native of Connecticut, came to California around 1846, and by 1850 married Martina Villard, the daughter of Lt. Francisco Villard and Susana Venegas. Villard had arrived at San Diego with Governor Jose Maria Echeandia in 1825. Brown first owned a farm at San Luis Rey and by 1850 the family was residing near the Bandini house at Old Town. Brown built a house which later became the Adobe Chapel at Old Town, and the family then resided in one of the last civilian houses at La Playa on Point Loma before the military took over that area.

George Allan Pendleton, a native of Bowling Green, Virginia and brother of Eugene Pendleton of New San Diego, arrived in California in 1847 with Stevenson's Regiment. On November 22, 1860 [N2/83], he married Maria Concepcion Estudillo, the granddaughter of Jose Maria Estudillo and Christobal Dominguez. The Pendletons lived at the Estudillo House and after her death, Pendleton married Clara Flynn, who later became Mrs. William Carson. They lived at the Derby-Pendleton House where Pendleton worked as County Clerk and Recorder until his death on March 5, 1871. Pendleton was buried at Protestant Cemetery in Old Town, a cemetery which no longer exists.

George Lyons, a native of Donegal, Ireland, arrived in California in 1847 or 1848, and in October, 1851, married Bernarda Villard, the sister of Martina Villard Brown. The Lyons owned a house at Old Town and a large garden in the San Diego River bed near Old Town.

Lt. Cave Johnson Couts, a native of Springfield, Tennessee and the son of William Couts and Nancy Johnson, arrived in California in 1848, and in 1849 produced one of the first surveys of Old Town and La Playa. On April 5, 1851, he married Maria Ysidora Barbara Bandini, the sister of Maria Arcadia Bandini Stearns, in the sala of the Bandini House at Old Town (N2/23). For a time, Cave Couts owned a hotel on Old Town Plaza, and the family resided at Rancho Guajome near Vista in North San Diego County. Cave Couts and Ysidora Bandini Couts are buried at Calvary Cemetery in Mission Hills.

George Alonzo Johnson, a native of Palatine Bridge, New York, arrived in California in 1848, and married Estefana Alvarado on June 4, 1859 at the Gila House Hotel in Old Town. She was the daughter of Francisco Maria Alvarado and Maria Tomasa Pico and the great granddaughter of Pedro Amador of the 1769 Expedition. The Johnsons moved to Arizona where Johnson owned one of the first steamboats on the Colorado River with his partner Alfred Henry Wilcox. Later the Johnsons lived at Rancho Penasquitos and at a wooden house on Old Town Plaza.

Henry Clayton, a native of England, arrived in San Diego around 1849 with the Boundary Commission, and was the first San Diego County surveyor. He married widow Maria Antonia Alvarado Snook in April, 1853 and they lived at Rancho Bernardo in North San Diego County.

Wiley Blount Couts, a native of Springfield, Tennessee, arrived in California around 1851, and married Maria del Refugio Concepcion Arguello on April 16, 1863 (N1/51) in the chapel at Rancho Guajome, the home of brother Cave Couts, in an apparent double ceremony with the Alfred Henry Wilcoxes. Refugio Couts and her sister were the granddaughters of Santiago Arguello and the great granddaughters of Jose Dario Arguello, who came to California with the Rivera expedition in 1781. The Wiley Couts family lived near Rancho Guajome in North San Diego County.

Alfred Henry Wilcox, a native of Middletown(?), Connecticut and the son of Alfred and Mary Wilcox, arrived in California in 1849 (notes of San Diego Genealogical Society). He married Maria Antonia Lugarda Eufemia Arguello, the sister of Mrs. Wiley Blount Couts, in an apparent double ceremony on April 16, 1863 in the chapel at Rancho Guajome (N1/51). The Wilcoxes became owners of Rancho La Punta and also built a large home in downtown San Diego.

Judge Benjamin Hayes of Baltimore, Maryland, the son of John Hayes and Maria Simmons, arrived in California by 1850, and after his wife Emily Chauncey died, he married Adelaida Serrano in 1866. She was a descendant of Francisco Serrano and Maria Balbaneda Silvas, who arrived at Presidio Hill in 1782. In his time at Old Town, Judge Hayes lived at the Rodriguez house, houses owned by the Serranos and lastly the Francisco Ruiz/Joaquin Carrillo House. He was buried at Old Calvary Cemetery in Los Angeles, a cemetery which no longer exists.

Andrew Cassidy, son of Marcus Cassidy and Catalina _____, was a native of County Cavan, Ireland, who came to California in 1853 and operated a tidal gauge at La Playa. He married Rosa Serrano, sister of Adelaida Serrano Hayes, on September 23, 1863. He acquired the Serrano's Pauma Rancho in North San Diego County, one of the sites associated with the Battle of San Pasqual during the Mexican War, and also owned the thousand acre Soledad Rancho in Sorrento Valley. When Rosa Serrano died, Andrew Cassidy married Maria Providencia Smith (see below).

There were seventeen men from the eastern seaboard, England or Ireland who married women of the Machado family. The Machados of Old Town descend from Jose Manuel Machado and Maria del Carmen Valenzuela, who arrived with the Rivera expedition in 1781. Their son, Joseph Manuel Machado married Maria Serafina Valdes, and four daughters: 1. Juana de Dios Machado; 2. Maria Antonia Juliana Machado; 3. Maria Guadalupe Ildefonsa Machado and 4. Rosa Maria Machado (all at N1/222) married as follows:

1. Juana de Dios Machado, baptized March 13, 1814 in San Diego, married first Damasio Alipas on August 22, 1829 on Presidio Hill. Their three daughters married the following men:

> Josefa Alipas married John Peters, possibly of Dublin, Ireland, the son of John and Josefina Peters, on April or September 24, 1850. They lived on a homestead at San Luis Rey and also ran a stage coach stop at Indian Wells.

> Ramona Alipas married William Curley in July, 1846? (date illegible). She married second ca. 1857 William "Cockney Bill" Williams, a native of England, who operated a hide house at La Playa for Henry Delano Fitch and then lived at Volcan Ranch, now Julian. They later operated a sheep ranch at Viejas.

> Maria Arcadia Alipas married Robert DeCatur Israel of Pittsburgh, PA, son of Joseph Israel and Anne Wilson, on August, 5, 1852. They lived near the Wrightingtons at Old Town, then at Point Loma lighthouse, where Israel was caretaker from 1871 to 1892.

Juana de Dios Machado married second Thomas Wrightington, a native of Fall River, Massachusetts and the son of John Wrightington and Dorothy Dvorak, on January 27, 1842. Their daughter, Maria Serafina Wrightington, married John S. Minter, a native of Missouri and possible son of William Minter and Rebecca Brundage, in 1859. The Minters lived near the Wrightingtons.

2. Maria Antonia Juliana Machado, baptized December 21, 1815 in San Diego, married Jose Antonio Nicasio Silvas around 1837 and they lived in the Machado-Silvas House on Old Town Plaza. When Maria Silvas became estranged from her husband, she may have obtained a civil divorce and married Enos Wall, a native of Freeport, Maine (date of marriage unknown).

Lorenza Silvas, the daughter of Maria Machado and Jose Silvas, married George Smith in 1860 (d. 1861), then Platt Huntington in 1865 (d. 1869), the son of John Huntington and Ana Brown. She then married Patrick O'Neill of Tyrone, Ireland by 1870, the son of Constantine O'Neill and Sarah Campbell, and they lived in a wooden house O'Neill built near the Machado-Silvas House.

3. Maria Guadalupe Ildefonsa Machado, baptized March 2, 1820 at San Diego, married first "Pedro Ball" or Peter V. Wilder of Boston, the son of Charles Wilder and Isabel Questin, on August 21, 1836, and they lived in a house across Mason Street from Juan Bandini's stables.

A daughter, Maria Dolores Wilder, married Dr. David Bancroft Hoffman, a native of New York and son of Chauncey and Mary Hoffman, on May 5, 1857. The Hoffmans lived in the Wilder house and Dr. Hoffman went on to become one of the founders of the San Diego County Medical Society. Another daughter, Maria Refugia Wilder, married Samuel Warren Hackett of Middleboro, Massachusetts, the son of Samuel Hackett and Augusta Cole, and a descendant of Richard Warren and John Alden of the *Mayflower*, on May 20, 1867. The Hacketts lived at La Playa.

After Peter Wilder died, Maria Guadalupe Ildefonsa Machado Wilder married Albert Benjamin Smith, a native of New York and son of Henry Smith and Betty Marshall, on November 23, 1850. The Smiths lived first at the Wilder house and then in a wooden house built by Smith just north of the Wrightington House. Their daughter, Maria Providencia Smith, married Andrew Cassidy, the widower of Rosa Serrano (discussed above).

4. Rosa Maria Machado, born November 15, 1828, married on February 3, 1845 John Collins Stewart, b. September 3, 1811 at Hallowell, Kennebec County, Maine, son of Solomon Freeman Stewart and Margaret Drew. They lived at the Machado-Stewart House west of Old Town Plaza. Their daughter Maria Nieves Stewart married Paul Connors, whose parents came from Virginia.

William Smythe discusses Americans who came early to Old Town in his *History of San Diego*, pp. 266-294. The following men were listed in Smythe (names in parentheses are those of the Hispanic families that the men married into or were related to): Julian Ames (Espinoza), Joshua H. Bean, Capt. J.C. Bogart, Thomas Henry Bush, Andrew Cassidy (Serrano/Machado), Henry Clayton (Alvarado), James W. Connors (Machado), Cave Johnson Couts (Bandini), Philip Crosthwaite (Lopez), William Curley (Machado), Thomas R. Darnell, A.S. Ensworth, William C. Ferrell, Lewis A. Franklin, Henry Delano Fitch (Carrillo), John Forster (Pico), J.R. Gitchell, Andrew Gray, Robert W. Groom, John Hays, Dr. David B. Hoffman (Machado),

Also Captain Robert D. Israel (Machado), Capt. George A. Johnson (Alvarado), Robert Kelly, Daniel Brown Kurtz, George Lyons (Villar), Joseph S. Mannasse, James McCoy, John Minter (Machado), William H. Moon, Ephraim Weed Morse, Charles P. Noell, William H. Noyes, George Allan Pendleton (Estudillo), Charles Henry Poole, James W. Robinson, Louis Rose, Marcus Schiller, Joshua Sloane, Albert Benjamin Smith (Machado), John Collins Stewart (Machado), Thomas W. Sutherland, George P. Tebbitts, Enos A. Wall (Machado), Jonathan T. Warner (married the daughter of William Alden Gale), Thomas Whaley, Peter Wilder (Machado), Oliver S. Witherby and Thomas Wrightington/Ridington (Machado).

The above men were instrumental in developing a new way of life in San Diego as the community came under American rule. Consult *Journal of San Diego History* articles, biographies and other sources at the San Diego Historical Society, the California Room of the San Diego Public Library, and other archives discussed below for more information about their lives.

For example, a *Journal of San Diego History* article was written about the elopment and marriage of Henry Delano Fitch and Josefa Carrillo and the reaction of the Hispanic community to this marriage in 1829. The article is entitled "A California Romance in Perspective: The Elopement, Marriage and Ecclesiastical Trial of Henry D. Fitch and Josefa Carrillo," JSDH Vol. XIX, No. 2 (April 1973).

Later Immigrant Groups
Germans and other nationality groups who arrived in San Diego can be traced through census records, voter registers and naturalization papers, which cite country of birth. See also Elizabeth MacPhail's book *The Influence of German Immigrants on the Growth of San Diego*, which discusses some of the German and Jewish settlers who came to San Diego.

There is a multi-volume set of books entitled *Germans in America* which is available at the Genealogy Room of the downtown San Diego Public Library and also at the Family History Center. These volumes list individuals who arrived on passenger ships from ca. 1850 on and includes their proposed destinations. Other nationality groups were also included in the first ten volumes of these books.

There is a book about early Jewish settlers in San Diego entitled *Old Town, New Town: An Enjoyment of San Diego Jewish History*, edited by William Kramer and Stanley and Laurel Schwartz. The book discusses various Jewish leaders, namely Lewis Polock, Louis Rose, Sig Steiner, Heyman Mannasse, Marcus Schiller, Mark Jacobs, and Isadore Louis. The book also describes the founding of Temple Beth Israel, the earliest Jewish temple in San Diego, the first temple building of which is now at Heritage Park near Old Town. A book about 1850s Old Town edited by Sylvia Arden, *Diary of a San Diego Girl*, features the diary of Victoria Jacobs and her fiancee Maurice Franklin, owner of the Franklin House hotel.

Additionally, there are *Journal of San Diego History* articles about early Jewish leaders of San Diego, including: "90 Years in San Diego: The Story of K.W." (Klauber Wangenheim Company), JSDH Vol. V, No. 3 (July 1959); "The Rose of San Diego" (Louis Rose), JSDH Vol. XIX, No. 4 (October 1973); "The Uneasy Alliance: Jewish-Anglo Relations in San Diego, 1850-1860," JSDH, Vol. XX, No. 3 (July 1974); and another article about Klauber Wangenheim in JSDH Vol. XXIX, No. 1 (January 1983).

Regarding Italian immigrants, there is a thesis entitled "India Street and Beyond: A History of the Italian Community of San Diego, 1850-1980," by Canice Ciruzzi, located at San Diego Historical Society. There is a *Journal of San Diego History* article on San Diego's Italian fishermen, JSDH Vol. XXVII, No. 4 (October 1981); and an article on tuna fishing from 1937-1941, JSDH Vol. XXXVII, No. 3 (July 1991).

For Portuguese immigrants, see "Culture and Education in Comunidade: The Portuguese-American Community in San Diego, California," by Craig Dale Rocha, located at United States International University (USIU).

A thesis entitled: "Mayor of Chinatown: The Life of Ah Quin," by Andrew Griego is located at the San Diego Historical Society. Murray K. Lee of the San Diego Chinese Historical Museum discussed the diaries of Ah Quin at a symposium held by the Congress of History, and the San Diego Historical Society has a copy of these diaries. There is also a thesis at San Diego Historical Society by Judith Liu entitled "Celestials in the Golden Mountain: The Chinese in One California City, San Diego 1870-1900."

There are *Journal of San Diego History* articles about the early Chinese of San Diego, namely: "The Chinese at Sorrento," JSDH Vol. X, No. 1 (January 1964); "San Diego History--The 'Chinaman's Struggle,'"

JSDH Vol. XX, No. 2 (April 1974); and articles about the San Diego Chinese Mission, JSDH Vol. XXIII, No. 2 (April 1977); Chinese fishermen 1870-1893, JSDH Vol. XXIII, No. 4 (October 1977); and a personal account of Ah Quin's experience as a labor contractor in 1884, JSDH Vol. XXV, No. 4 (October 1979).

A publication of Dr. Ray Brandes at the downtown San Diego Public Library entitled *San Diego's Chinatown and Stingaree District* discusses an archeological dig that Dr. Brandes conducted in this district in 1985. This publication gives an excellent history of San Diego's Chinatown. Chinese individuals and families are also listed in the census from 1850 on.

There are two theses at San Diego State University about the Japanese experience, namely: "Japanese American Associations in San Diego," by Sakiko Akita; and "The Issei Farmer and the California Alien Land Act in San Diego County, 1900-1942," by Thomas Carnes.

Journal of San Diego History articles about the Japanese experience include: "The Internment of the Japanese of San Diego County During the Second World War," JSDH Vol. XVIII, No. 1 (January 1972); an article on Kondo Masaharu, fisherman, JSDH Vol. XXIII, No. 3 (July 1977); an article on Japanese in San Diego before the war, JSDH Vol. XXIV, No. 4 (July 1978); an article on the relocation of San Diego's Nikkei community in 1942, JSDH Vol. XXXIX, Nos. 1-2, (Winter/Spring 1993); and another article about the same subject in JSDH, Vol. 42, No. 3 (Summer 1996). There is also an article about Philippinos in San Diego, JSDH Vol. XXII, No. 3 (July 1976).

The first individual to arrive at San Diego with African ancestry was Sebastian Manriquez, who came to San Diego on May 14, 1769 with the Rivera overland expedition. Another man with African ancestry, Juan Antonio Coronel, arrived at San Diego with the Portola/Serra overland expedition on July 1, 1769. As early as 1848, two black men, Alan Light and Richard Freeman, owned a store on Old Town Plaza. Light's story is chronicled in "A Black American in Mexican San Diego," JSDH Vol. XX, No. 2 (April 1974). Problems of racial prejudice in Old Town during that time period are reflected in "The Mary Walker Incident: Black Prejudice in San Diego, 1866," JSDH Vol. XIX, No. 2 (April 1973).

In the 1880 census, black individuals and families appeared in outlying areas like Julian and the back country. The 1890 census was destroyed, so the next census year which reflects the black presence in San Diego is the 1900 census and census returns for each decade thereafter, where race was listed along with age, marital status, nativity, and other information. The Family History Center has census returns on microfilm for all years up to 1920 and portions of 1930, and it is a good place to view the census microfilms to trace the black presence in San Diego.

Black migration increased greatly in the late 1880's with the coming of the railroad, and one can determine which individuals were in San Diego during the 1880s by burials at Mount Hope, the city owned cemetery, where many black individuals were buried in Section 2. The San Diego Genealogical Society has published a book listing individuals who were buried at Mount Hope from 1869 to 1909, and is now publishing information about burials after 1909 in *Leaves and Saplings*. As race was one element of information collected by the cemetery, it could be determined that 147 black individuals were buried at Mount Hope from 1869 to 1909. The Mount Hope burial book is for sale by the San Diego Genealogical Society, and their address and meeting schedule are given elsewhere in this book.

Additional *Journal of San Diego History* articles about the black experience in San Diego include an article on blacks in San Diego County, JSDH Vol. XXI, No. 4 (October 1975); an article by Larry Malone on blacks in San Diego, JSDH Vol. XXVII, No. 2 (April 1981) which was also republished as *Black Pioneers in San Diego: 1880-1920*, available for purchase at the San Diego Historical Society. An article on the history of Logan Heights was published in JSDH Vol. XXIX, No. 1 (January 1983). There were also the following additional articles, one on Camp Lockett, JSDH Vol. XXXIX, Nos. 1-2 (Winter/Spring 1993); and an oral history interview of Bert Ritchey, JSDH Vol. 42, No. 2 (Spring 1996).

In addition, there are three theses available at the San Diego Historical Society, one by LeRoy Harris entitled "The Other Side of the Freeway: A Study of Settlement Patterns of Negroes and Mexican Americans in San Diego"; another by Robert Carlton entitled "Blacks in San Diego County, 1850-1900"; and another entitled "Ethnic and Racial Violence in San Diego 1880-1920." There is also a biography of George Washington Woodbey, an early Black Socialist leader in San Diego who gained national recognition, which is at the California room of the downtown San Diego Public Library.

The Black Historical Society is located at 906 Market Street, San Diego, CA, 92101, and has a research library containing genealogical materials and other items documenting the history of San Diego's black community, including deeds, property records, census records and directories. The organization also has books, posters and videos for sale and conducts tours. The Black Historical Society's web address is www.blackhistoricalsociety.com. The head of this organization is Karen Huff, whose e-mail address is karen@blackhistoricalsociety.com. Their mailing address is P.O. Box 122469, San Diego, CA 92112-2469. Their phone number is (619) 685-7215 and their fax number is (619) 667-9431.

Theses about Prominent People
At times, there will be theses written about prominent San Diego figures. In "Preliminary Checklist of Master's Theses and Doctoral Dissertations on the History of San Diego," the following theses were listed. Note that entries with an asterisk indicate theses also in the archives of the San Diego Historical Society. Also note that there are now more theses in these libraries than were on this "Preliminary Checklist."

Theses at University of San Diego discuss: Belle Baranceanu, Walter C. Bellou(*), Maria Amparo Ruiz de Burton(*), Cave Couts, Phil Crosthwaite(*), Rev. Clarence Damschroeder, Edward Heath Davis, Don Juan Forster, Samuel Wood Hamill(*), Judge Benjamin F. Hayes, William Sterling Hebbard(*), Samuel P. Heintzelman, Eugene Hoffman(*), Robert Decatur Israel and Richard Kerren.

There are also theses at University of San Diego on William and Marion Kettner(*), Sigmund Lubin(*), Ricardo Flores Magon, John Bankhead Magruder, John Mortenson, Edward Quale(*), the Reid Brothers(*), Dr. Peter Charles Remondino, Richard Requa, Lillian Jenette Rice(*), Edward Willis Scripps, Thomas W. Sweeney, Theophile Verlaque(*), Sebastian Viscaino, Hazel Wood Waterman, Olaf Weighorst, Amiel Weeks Whipple, Charles William(*), Don Benito Wilson (2 theses), and Judge Oliver S. Witherby(*).

Theses at San Diego State University discuss: Charlotte Baker(*), Cave Couts(*), Robert Patterson Effinger(*), Alonzo E. Horton(*), Frank Kimball(*), George White Marston(*), Anson Peaslee Mill(*), Ephraim W. Morse(*), Ah Quin, Malcom J. Rogers, Ellen Browning Scripps(*), Governor Robert Whitney Waterman(*), Thomas Whaley and Bob Wilson.

Thesis at University of Southern California discusses: Henry Delano Fitch(*).

Additional Pedigree Charts
Pedigree charts other than those mentioned for the Old Town Spanish families are also available in San Diego. The Family History Center has a volume entitled *San Diego Pedigrees*, which is a compilation of conated pedigrees of San Diegans, including about 500 pages of pedigree charts and a 26 page index.

The San Diego Genealogical Society requests that each new member donate a pedigree chart tracing four generations of the families that they descend from. These are arranged alphabetically in file cabinets at the San Diego Genealogical Society Library in El Cajon and are noted in their card catalog. Pedigree charts are often included in the Biographical Files at the San Diego Historical Society.

You can also downloaded pedigree charts from computers at your local Family History Center. The computers are probably best to use after you have traced your family back several generations, for only then will you be able to connect with research done by others on earlier generations of your family. These pedigree charts can also be accessed online. Go to www.familysearch.com on the Internet and click on "Search". If you do connect to earlier research while using the familysearch computer, there is a chance that you might go back several generations or more, which will greatly facilitate your work. But always be careful to check the accuracy of work done by others.

HOUSE HISTORIES/HISTORICAL SITE BOARD REPORTS

One way to find out about your family is to conduct research about the houses they lived in. First, find out when your family arrived in San Diego by using census returns, voter registers, land records, tax records or newspaper reports. Then the following steps could be undertaken to conduct a house history:

1. Determine the exact address where your family lived by consulting local City Directories, published from the late 1800s to about 1980. These are located at the California Room of the downtown San Diego Public Library or at the San Diego Historical Society. Go through the City Directories year by year to find out how long your family lived at a particular address.

2. Use "reverse City Directories," published in the City Directories from 1926 on to help you locate other members of your family who may have lived on the same street as your ancestor did. Reverse City Directories are listed by street name followed by the names of individuals who lived up and down a particular street.

3. Go to the County Assessor's Office to determine the present owners of the property you are interested in. Conduct a title search to see who the past owners were by tracing old deeds on microfilm at the County Assessor's Office. The address of the County Assessor's office is presented later in this book.

4. Visit the property to see if the house you are interested in is still standing. Talk to the present owners to determine if they know the history of the house. Some addresses changed from time to time, and some houses were moved or relocated. The Historical Society has lot books from 1890-1930, listing lot descriptions and property owner's names.

5. If the house is located in one of the older sections of San Diego (Golden Hill, Downtown, East Village, the Gaslamp Quarter, the Chinese district, Little Italy, Middletown, Old Town, Banker's Hill or Mission Hills), find out if the house has been declared a historic site by contacting the City of San Diego Historical Site Board. The address of the Historical Site Board is presented later in this book.

The San Diego Historical Society and the California Room also have Historic Site Board Reports, and the California Room additionally has a recent survey of old houses in downtown and parts of Middletown. There are also house books like one published by Karen Johl on Victorian homes in San Diego which is available at the San Diego Public Library. The Johl book provides some information on the past owners of the Victorian houses featured in the book.

6. There may be photos and architectural plans for your house at the San Diego Historical Society. Also, photos of houses and/or proposed house plans often appear in old newspaper articles, and these can be viewed on microfilm at the Newspaper Room of the downtown San Diego Public Library. An index to people, places and events discussed in local newspapers is available in the California Room of the downtown San Diego Public Library for the years 1851 to 1903 and 1930 to 1983. If you know the name of a prior owner or architect who designed the house you are interested in, the indexes may help you find news articles that may have a photo of the structure.

Photos can document changes in a house and in the surrounding property. Pay close attention to the growth of foliage around the house as this could help to date a photo and the house depicted in it. Photos may also show those who lived in the house, and you also might run across a photo of a relative by doing a house history.

Also check the San Diego Historical Society photo archives for photos of your family, or of a house owned by your family or by a prior owner, or under an architect's name. The San Diego Historical Society photo archives has the largest collection of historical photos in the San Diego area. There are also photos in the biographical and subject files at both the San Diego Historical Society and the California Room of the downtown public library.

7. Maps are also very useful. Sanborn fire insurance maps in book or microfilm format are available at the Newspaper and California Rooms of the downtown San Diego Public Library and at the San Diego Historical Society. These show how the neighborhood in which the house you are interested in developed over time. Sanborn Maps are available for 1887, 1888, 1904, 1921, with later updates into the 1940s and beyond.

Obtain subdivision maps from the County Administration Building, second floor, which show how property in the city was subdivided. Older maps which show San Diego prior to subdivision are featured in a book entitled *Maps to the Pueblo Lands of San Diego 1602-1874* by Neal Harlow, which is at the California Room of the downtown public library.

The Pourade books mentioned above have many maps of San Diego, as does the Elizabeth MacPhail book *The Story of New San Diego and of Its Founder Alonzo E. Horton*. Also check the San Diego Historical Society, with its excellent map collection, and old maps at the County Administration Building, 2400 Pacific Highway, 1st Floor.

8. Lot books are available at the San Diego Historical Society from 1890 to 1930. Lot books contain yearly property assessments for individuals and the acreage, value of improvements, and mortgage number for the properties.

9. Finally, round out your study by doing further reading about the area in which your family lived. There are books about Old Town and many other San Diego communities which explore how the communities developed and who lived there. Perhaps your family is mentioned and/or depicted in these books.

The study of house histories might include the study of unusual fixtures or features that adorned a house. For years, Alonzo Horton, called the "Father of San Diego," had two lion statues which guarded the entrance to his home at 1929 First Avenue.

The lions roamed after Horton moved out. They were purchased by Albert Wuest from Thomas Daley, a subsequent owner of 1929 First Avenue, and for a time Mr. Wuest had them at his former home at 3018 State Street in South Mission Hills. They were then moved to a later home owned by Mr. Wuest at 3029 Union Street, and there they remain to this day. Urns from the old Horton home at 1929 First Avenue are now located at 3013 Horton Avenue.

Sites where famous people lived often become historic sites, and a report is made during the designation process which justifies the historical designation. The San Diego Historical Site Board maintains a set of reports which describes the various buildings, sites and locations that have attained "historic site" status. Descriptive data in the Historical Site Board Reports includes the name of the site, its location, its current and original ownership, original use and period (such as "Early American Period"), physical details of the property, a summary of its historic significance, a map showing site location, and photographs of the property, along with other supplemental information where available.

Originals of these reports are housed at the Historical Site Board at the City Administration Building in downtown San Diego. A call to the City Planning Department will access the Historical Site Board. Their phone number is: (619) 235-5200. As mentioned above, copies of these reports are also kept at the San Diego Historical Society and at the California Room of the downtown San Diego Public Library.

Another interesting thing to consider is whether the house you are researching was a prefabricated house. Prefabricated buildings were being erected in San Diego since the first hide house warehouses were put up at La Playa in 1829. There were at least 16 prefabricated houses brought to "New Town" San Diego by 1850 from San Francisco, and one of these, the William Heath Davis House, still exists and can be toured at the Gaslamp Quarter in downtown San Diego.

Perhaps the house you are researching is a Sears Roebuck catalog prefabricated house, some of which were also erected in San Diego. Betsy Green, in *Discovering the History of Your House and Your Neighborhood*, (Santa Monica: Santa Monica Press, 2002), pp. 63-64, discusses Sears Roebuck houses and states: "From 1908 to 1940, Sears, Roebuck & Company sold approximately 100,000 homes by catalog. There were about 450 different styles--from large to small. Houses ranged from modest cottages, to farmhouses, to elaborate Colonial Revival homes. All the pieces of the home were shipped by rail, so you can find Sears houses wherever you can find a railroad...

"All of the lumber was cut to size at the factory. ... Every piece of lumber in a Sears house had a number stamped on it, and assembly was required. ... Many people learn that they have a catalog house when they or a contractor tear things apart and find numbered pieces.

"Some Sears houses have plumbing fixtures or other pieces of hardware with the Sears name on it or simply 'SR.' Occasionally people find a shipping label from Sears attached to a board in the attic or basement."[9] So if your house was built from 1908 to 1940, check to see if it was a Sears Roebuck catalog house.

FAMILY HISTORY RESEARCH LOCATIONS IN SAN DIEGO
We now come to a listing of major research libraries to visit when conducting family history research in San Diego. Sometimes these resources will only be used for a specific purpose, like going to the county to obtain a birth record. Other locations contain a variety of records, so it is wise to make a plan when visiting these locations to get as much as you can out of your visit there. The major research locations in San Diego include the following:

San Diego Historical Society
P.O. Box 81825, San Diego, CA 92138. Phone: (619) 232-6203. Archivist: Dennis Sharp. Curator of Photographs: Greg Williams. Hours: Weds-Sat, 10-4:30. This collection can be accessed online by typing "San Diego Historical Society" into Google or another Internet search engine.

The San Diego Historical Society archives and photo collection is physically located in the Casa de Balboa on El Prado, just west of the Reuben H. Fleet Space Theater in Balboa Park. The Historical Society has many genealogical resources which will be discussed more fully under the heading "Specific Genealogical Records Available in San Diego."

At the archives, there are three card catalogs: one available to researchers and an older card catalog in back which is not accessible to patrons but can be accessed by the archivist or his assistants, and it is good to access this catalog because it has a great deal of information. There is also a computerized catalog which researchers can use. These three catalogs contain many citations to individuals, county histories, journal articles, oral history interviews, and other source materials of use to researchers.

Two of the most important genealogical sources at the Historical Society archives are the Biographical Files and the Vertical Files. The Biographical Files contain over 260 notebooks of newspaper clippings on individuals, arranged alphabetically by surname. The Vertical Files contain 1,300 folders of clippings arranged alphabetically for over 700 subjects. Both collections are continually being updated by the Historical Society staff and volunteers.

The main publication of the San Diego Historical Society is the *Journal of San Diego History*. In 1975, an index to Volumes 1 through 20 of the *Journal of San Diego History* was published, indexing articles from 1955 through 1974. The index can be purchased at the Historical Society bookstore and at the Serra Museum on Presidio Hill. Back issues of the *Journal of San Diego History* can also be purchased at those locations and at used bookstores around San Diego such as Wahrenbrachs Books. An index to later volumes has not been published but is available for researchers to use at the Historical Society archives. Please note that the full text of *Journal of San Diego History* articles is also available on the website of the San Diego Historical Society.

Additional guide books or articles available at the Historical Society include the following:

>An article by Richard Crawford and others entitled "Local History Materials in the Research Archives of the San Diego Historical Society," *Journal of San Diego History* (Spring 1991).

>*A Guide to the San Diego Historical Society Public Records Collection*, by Richard Crawford, published in 1987. This publication is available from the San Diego Historical Society bookstore, and selected references will be made to this book in the "Specific Genealogical Records Available in San Diego" section below.

>Dennis Sharp, the current Historical Society archivist, has prepared an update to the above *Guide*, entitled "A Guide to the San Diego Historical Society Public Records Collection: 2001 Edition, Revised, Updated and Edited," *Journal of San Diego History*, Vol. 47, No.s 1 & 2, (Winter/Spring 2001). It includes the sources discussed by Rick Crawford but supplements them with additional public records received by the Historical Society since 1987. It is an invaluable guide to public records held by the Society, and should be consulted whenever you wish to access such records.

The photo collection of the San Diego Historical Society is located adjacent to the archives, and is the largest collection of its kind in the city. It dates from 1870 to the present and now totals over 2.5 million images of San Diego. The Historical Society obtained the photographs of the Title Insurance & Trust collection, those of many commercial and amateur photographers, and donated photos from local families, organizations and individuals. Included in the collection are photographs of people, landmarks, architecture, and historic events, plus negatives of photos which appeared in San Diego newspapers.

This collection has been described in a special edition of the *Journal of San Diego History*, Volume 44, (Spring/Summer 1998) entitled "Guide to the Photograph Collection of the San Diego Historical Society," by Greg Williams, photo curator. It can be purchased from the Historical Society, and it contains wonderful descriptions of the core collections and of photograph albums donated by people over the years. The guide is fully indexed, allowing a researcher to determine if their ancestors are among those who contributed photos to the collection.

San Diego Public Library
The central branch of the San Diego Public Library is located in downtown San Diego at 820 "E" Street, San Diego, CA 92101. Their hours are Monday and Wednesday, Noon to 8 p.m., Tuesday, Thursday, Friday and Saturday, 9:30 to 5:30, and Sunday 1-5. The main phone number is (619) 236-5800.

The Newspaper Room, California Room, and Genealogy Room are all located adjacent to each other on the second floor of the library, and information will be presented about the holdings of these collections under the heading "Specific Genealogical Resources in San Diego". If you come across an "RCC" designation in a call number when researching a book at the public library, it means that the book is located in the California Room. An "RGY" designation in the call number means that the book is located in the Genealogy Room. Books in these two rooms do not circulate.

There are a number of filing cabinets in the California Room which contain newspaper clippings, excerpts from magazines or journals, and possible citations to individuals, locations, historic sites, or events. There is a ring binder at the California Room which lists subject headings included in these filing cabinets.

The California Room also has an old card catalog with names of people in it and citations to journal articles and book biographies these people. It also covers many subjects and events, and locates little known locations in San Diego County. There are city directories for various years from the late 1880s to 1984, a marriage index on microfiche covering the entire state of California for 1960 through 1986, and a death index on microfiche covering the entire state of California from 1940 through 1995.

The Newspaper Room contains microfilm copies of the major newspapers in San Diego. This is the best place to view the microfilms for there are a number of reader/printers which can print out the text of a newspaper article or obituary. There is an index to newspaper articles for selected years in the California Room which will be discussed under the "Newspaper" heading below. Additionally, recent news articles from the *San Diego Union-Tribune* are now available on computer in the California Room from 1984 to the present (with a two-month time lag), which can be used to research specific names and/or subjects.

Mary Allely, former librarian for the California Room, wrote an article describing its holdings entitled: "Local History Materials in the California Room of the San Diego Public Library", *Journal of San Diego History* (Summer 1991) which will be helpful to researchers unfamiliar with the holdings in this collection.

The Genealogy Room contains a few books on San Diego history, namely county histories, printed census returns, and other such books. But the books on San Diego are for the most part located in the California room and in the History Department. For more information about the holdings of the Genealogy Room for other states, see "Taking Your Research Outside San Diego," below.

The History Department, on the first floor, contains books on California and San Diego history, accounts of individuals, and books about local histories of communities surrounding San Diego such as El Cajon, Ocean Beach, La Jolla, Spring Valley, Coronado, and Chula Vista. There are maps in the history department which can also facilitate your research. The card catalog of the San Diego Public Library can also be accessed online using Google or other search engines.

San Diego Family History Center
The Family History Center is located near National University in Mission Valley off Fairmont. The address is 4195 Camino Del Rio South, San Diego, CA 92108, and their phone is (619) 584-7668. Their hours are Monday, Tuesday, Friday and Saturday from 10 a.m. to 3 p.m. and Wednesday and Thursday from 10 a.m. to 8 p.m. The Family History Center has a number of books on San Diego history and has Marie Northrop's *Spanish-Mexican Families in Early California* and William Mason's *The Census of 1790*. It also has a number of cemetery books and census microfilms for all years and all states.

Books on San Diego history at the Family History Center are listed below under "Specific Genealogical Sources in San Diego." Please note that some of the publications of the San Diego Genealogical Society are housed at this location. For research outside of California, see more about the Family History Center below in the section entitled "Taking Your Research Outside San Diego."

San Diego Genealogical Society
This is the major organization for genealogical research in San Diego, and it has a large membership. Their mailing address and the location of their genealogical library is 1050 Pioneer Way, Suite E, El Cajon, CA. The phone number there is (619) 588-0065 (answering machine) and you can also access their website by typing in "San Diego Genealogical Society" on Google or another Internet search engine.

This group is very active in San Diego. Meetings of the group are held on the second Saturday of the month from noon to around 2:30 p.m. except for the month of January when the group holds its annual luncheon and the month of December. The monthly meeting is held at St. Dunstan's Episcopal Church, 6556 Park Ridge Boulevard, located in the San Carlos area near Patrick Henry Junior High School. Additionally, the group puts on an annual family history fair in the fall of each year, with speakers, book vendors, and so on.

The group publishes *Leaves and Saplings*, which presents information month after month that is important for researchers interested in San Diego history, including military, cemetery, hospital and other records. An *Index to San Diego Leaves and Saplings, 1974-1985* is available at the Family History Center, and additionally about 20 volumes of *Leaves and Saplings* dating from Winter of 1973 to January/March of 1989 are located there. The publications which this organization has for sale include the following:

The 1850, 1860 and 1870 Federal Census for San Diego County (each in separate volumes).

The 1852 California State Census for San Diego County

Land Records for San Diego County: Grantor Index to Deed Books A-E and 1-25, (1850-1875)

Newspaper Records: Vital Records from San Diego Newspapers, May 1851-Feb 1885

Taxpayers, San Diego County, 1850-1852

Tax Assessment Rolls for San Diego County, 1853-1863

Index to Pre-Emption Claims, San Diego County, (from 1850-1890s)

Birth Records, San Diego County, (from 1860-1889)

Church Records for First Presbyterian Church, San Diego (most dates from 1900).

Episcopal Church Records: Holy Trinity Episcopal and St. Pauls Episcopal (records of 194 baptisms from 1872-1887; 82 marriages and 89 burials from 1873-1887, a list of 189 communicants from 1872-1883 and 788 communicants on Easter Day, 1887, plus an index).

Great Register of Voters, San Diego County, 1866-1879

Coroner's Inquests of San Diego County, 1871-1896

Johnson Saum and Nobel Mortuary Records: 1869-February 1888, 1907-1909

Mount Hope Cemetery Burial Records, Volume 1, 1869-1909. Vol. 2 is currently being published in San Diego Genealogical Society's *Leaves and Saplings*

Escondido Cemetery Records, 1883-1960

San Diego Cemetery and Burial Records (cemetery and burial records for Rancho de la Nation/La Vista Cemetery, National City, CA; five pp. San Pasqual records for deaths 1877-1970s.

This organization has its own library in El Cajon, and membership in the group allows you to use the library at all hours of the day or night. Non-members can visit the library on Thursdays, but call first to find out the hours that the library is open.

The library is a wonderful resource if you are branching from local history to the history of your family in other locations. Pedigree charts submitted by members of this organization are cataloged alphabetically in the card catalog and in file cabinets. They also have a tremendous number of newsletters and journals from genealogical societies around the country which are invaluable for tracing individuals because they contain tombstone inscriptions from little known cemeteries, church, and other records. There are also genealogical magazines at this library and some city directories and maps.

A good resource at this library for San Diego research is a full run of *Leaves and Saplings* issues and also the San Diego Genealogical Society newsletter. The California holdings in this library are limited to the same types of books that are available at San Diego Public Library and its branches, but the library has *Journal of San Diego History* volumes from the earliest volume to volumes published ten years ago.

Public Records
Public records--birth, marriage, divorce, civil, criminal, death and probate--provide primary evidence of the existence of a person. They normally can be treated with some confidence except that they are products of human endeavor, and may have the inevitable misspelled names and wrong dates. Be sure to check all source information against other information to pin down exact dates of events you are researching.

Birth, marriage, property, and death records are located at the County Assessor/Recorder/Clerk's Office, County Administration Building, 1600 Pacific Highway, San Diego, CA 92101. Hours: M-F, 8-5. Phone: (619) 237-0502. Information about this office can be obtained by accessing the San Diego County Assessor/Recorder/Clerk's website using Google or another Internet search engine.

A recent County policy (1/2003) regarding vital records stated that no <u>indexes</u> for birth, marriage and death records would be made available to the public after the passage of Senate Bill 1614, which prohibited public records repositories from providing index information due to the abuse of such records by commercial entities. See more about county vital records in the "Specific Genealogical Records Available" section of this book.

The following property records are available online at the website of the County Assessor/Recorder/Clerk:

Real Estate Index, Alpha	1982 - present
Real Estate Index, Numeric	1982 - present
Real Estate Index, Alpha	1970 - present (an additional index that was compiled)
Assessor/Tax Collector	Current only

Civil, criminal, divorce, and probate records are filed at 220 West Broadway, San Diego, CA 92101. Most family history research will be done in Older Records, which is located in the basement of this building. Hours: M-F, 9-4:30. Phone: (619) 531-3244.

Californians voted to combine Municipal Courts and Superior Courts into a "Superior Court" system and the records of the former Municipal Courts are now housed elsewhere. Municipal Court records are purged when they are ten years old and no "Older Records" department exists for these records, apparently. Thus eventually there will no longer be any "Municipal Court" records to access.

Office of the County Historian
Lynne Christenson, the County Historian, works for the County Department of Parks and Recreation Environmental Education Office, located at 4370 Sweetwater Road, Bonita, CA 91902. Her phone number is (619) 472-2734, and her fax number is (619) 472-7575. Lynne Christenson can also be reached at lchrispk@co.san-diego.ca.us The archives of the County Historian contain information about the County parks system and about historic buildings included in them. For example, a large collection of information is available about Rancho Guajome and its owner Cave Johnson Couts. Contact the Office of the County Historian for further information about their holdings and hours of operation.

San Diego County Public Law Library
The San Diego County Public Law Library is located at 1105 Front Street, San Diego, CA 92101. Ph: (619) 685-6553. Pat Lopez is the curator of the historical collection. Their hours are M-Th: 8 a.m. to 6:00 p.m., Friday: 8-5, and Saturday, 10-5. Access their website by typing in San Diego County Public Law Library on Google or another Internet search engine.

The Law Library has biographies, folders of newspaper clippings and photos of local attorneys and judges, Grand Jury and Justice Court files, files on the Colorado River water litigation, the *San Diego Daily Transcript* newspaper, old appellate court briefs from San Diego and California, a "Pioneer Room" which contains book collections of local attorneys, and books with biographies of local attorneys. Contact Pat Lopez for further information on this collection.

The Congress of History of San Diego
The Congress of History was formed as a networking group to bring together representatives of all of the major historical societies in San Diego and Imperial Counties. This means that there may be a member of the Congress of History who has a great deal of information about a particular community of interest to you.

Meetings of the Congress of History are held at members' museums throughout the county and the meeting locations are given in their publication, *Adelante*. The Congress of History website at www.congressofhistory.org only has a calendar with the dates of the meetings, but no meeting locations.

Regular meetings of the Congress of History are held on the third Saturday of January, February, May, July, September and November, with their annual meeting being held in February. Helen Halmay is the contact person for information about the group's newsletter. Please access their website for her address.

Catholic Archives
The Halter Library is a research library for the Catholic Diocese of San Diego, and it is located at Mission San Diego de Alcala, 10818 San Diego Mission Road, San Diego, CA, 92108. Their phone number is (619) 283-6338. The library is only open to the public on Tuesday and Thursday from 10:00 a.m. until noon, and during their regular hours there are several people available to assist patrons.

The library has genealogical information for many of the early Hispanic families of San Diego that was compiled by the late Sr. Catherine Louise LaCoste. The library has early mission histories, information on priests who staffed the early missions, the Fr. Francis J. Weber books on California missions and other Catholic historical topics, subject files on a variety of topics, and general books and journals on San Diego history.

The archives also has original records of Indian and Spanish baptisms, marriages and burials in old mission record books which can only be accessed by head librarian Janet Bartel. The records center for more recent records of the Catholic Diocese of San Diego, including birth, marriage and death records on microfilm and other information, is not open to the public. The address of this records center is: Catholic Diocese of San Diego, 3888 Paducah Drive, San Diego, CA, and their phone number is (858) 490-8200.

Upcoming Genealogy Events
The Computer Genealogy Society of San Diego publishes an online "Detailed Calendar of Events" which discusses upcoming events of genealogical interest in San Diego, including seminars and classes on genealogy. The calendar has information about genealogical libraries in San Diego, North San Diego County and several libraries in Los Angeles and gives their hours of operation and location. This website also contains links to other groups and lists the addresses of all Family History Centers in the San Diego area. Contact the Computer Genealogy Society website at cgssd.org to access this calendar of events.

SPECIFIC GENEALOGICAL RECORDS AVAILABLE
We now come to specific records you will find at the various research locations mentioned above. They include the following: **PLEASE NOTE: all citations in bold below, flagged with a "PRC" and a page number, are direct quotes from Richard Crawford's *A Guide to the San Diego Historical Society Public Records Collection* (San Diego: San Diego Historical Society, 1987).** Again, consult Dennis Sharp's new, edited, and revised edition of this Guide when doing research into public records. For more information about this new guide, see the main entry for "San Diego Historical Society" above.

Baptisms/Birth Records
The earliest baptisms of the Catholic Church occurred on Presidio Hill and at Mission San Diego de Alcala, and details of these baptisms are available in two books by R. Clinton Griffin which were compiled using records from the Catholic archives and with the help of the late Sr. Catherine Louise LaCoste:

Mission San Diego de Alcala Baptisms, 1769-1799, which is at the San Diego Historical Society.

Mission San Diego de Alcala Baptisms for the Mission and Vicinity: 1769-1850, which is at the downtown San Diego Public Library.

These were the earliest baptisms that occurred in San Diego. The books contain the date of baptism and the name of the child or adult being baptized along with the names of the parents and godparents, where available. At times a birth date or year of birth can be interpolated for the record will read "an infant 15 days old" or "an adult Indian about 20 years old." The above books are fully indexed for every name that appears in the baptismal record, with the names of those being baptized flagged in bold type. In most instances only the first names of Indians being baptized are given although at times their parents or spouses are listed with their full names. Unlike the early burial records where there were gaps in the burial record numbers, the baptismal records appear to be complete for every baptism that took place.

The first record book to 1799 contains mostly a record of Indian baptisms, but there are also 133 baptisms of children of the early Hispanic soldiers who lived on Presidio Hill. Regarding those baptisms, three children were baptized for the Alanis, Monroy, Olivera, Pico, Silvas, Sotelo, Verdugo and Zuniga families; four were baptized for the Feliz, Gil, Lisalde, Rosas, Rubio, Sepulveda and Ybarra (Ibarra) families; five for the Alvarez, Leiva, Ortega, Romero and Yorba families, six for the Valenzuela family and seven for the Lopez family, which accounts for 90 (68%) of the Hispanic children being baptized. The second baptism book (from 1800 to 1850) contains mostly the baptisms of Hispanic children.

The census for San Diego from 1850 and every ten years thereafter lists children living in households by name and age. Thus the census is a primary tool not only for discovering the existence of children but also for ascertaining the approximate year they were born and who their parents and siblings were. The San Diego Genealogical Society has for sale the 1850, 1860 and 1870 Federal Census enumerations for San Diego County and the 1852 California State Census for San Diego county.

The San Diego Genealogical Society has a publication for sale entitled: *Newspaper Records: Vital Records from San Diego Newspapers, May 1851-Feb 1885* and this publication is also available at the Family

History Center. The publication includes birth information from the *San Diego Herald*, the earliest newspaper in San Diego, from September 9, 1854 to February 26, 1859, and birth information from the *San Diego Union* from February 20, 1869 to February 13, 1885. The book is fully indexed.

Regarding church records of births, the San Diego Genealogical Society has for sale a publication entitled *Episcopal Church Records: Holy Trinity Episcopal and St. Pauls Episcopal* which documents baptisms at Holy Trinity Episcopal Church from July 17, 1872 to June 20, 1886 (185 baptisms) and at St. Pauls Episcopal from December 25, 1884 to February 2, 1887 (eight baptisms). Other early churches in San Diego could be contacted to determine if they have records of baptisms. See Ben Dixon's *San Diego Religious Heritage* and William Smythe's *History of San Diego* at the downtown San Diego Public Library which discuss early San Diego churches.

Additional records are available for earlier times. The San Diego Historical Society has a group of records from the County Recorder entitled:

> **Quarterly Returns of Marriages and Births. 1858-1860. PRC, p. 38. Returns of birth show name, sex, and color of newborn; date and location of birth; names, residence, color, and nativity of parents, and date of recordation. Arranged chronologically; indexed by name.**

The Historical Society has another group of records from the same source called:

> **Return of Birth. 1874-1876. PRC, p. 38. Birth notices show the name, sex, and race of the newborn; date and place of birth; name and residence of parents; names of medical attendant and person making report. Arranged chronologically by date of birth and indexed by name.**

Birth records are available at San Diego County from 1873 to 1904 in old books in the vault and from 1905 to the present on computer and on microfiche. Birth records are not open to the public and cannot be accessed on the county computer system or online. They are available only to the individual in question, their families, or to those who have permission from the families to obtain the records for them. People who wish to purchase birth records must have the information necessary to locate the record. Call San Diego County for additional information on birth records at (619) 237-0502.

Naturalization Records

A study was not done on naturalization records for purposes of this book, but the following is a brief survey of the types of records that are available. The downtown San Diego Public Library has an "Index to Declaration of Intention [to be naturalized] in the Superior Court of San Diego County, California, 1853-1956" on microfilm in the California Room. It also has "Naturalization Index Cards from the Superior Court of San Diego County, CA, 1920-1956" on five reels of microfilm in the California Room.

The National Archives in Laguna Niguel (discussed at the end of this book) has the following naturalization records for San Diego:

Index to San Diego Superior Court Naturalizations, 1929-1956, microfilm M1526 VI

Index to Citizens Naturalized, San Diego Superior Court, 1853-1956, microfilm M1609 VI

San Diego Superior Court Records, 1883-1940, microfilm M1613 VI

Index to San Diego Superior Court Declarations, 1853-1956, microfilm M1612 VI

Declarations of Intent to the San Diego Superior Court, 1871-1941, microfilm 9L-RA-1 VI

The Family History Center has many records on naturalization which are too numerous to mention here. Visit the Family History Center for additional information on naturalization records and for pamphlets which can be purchased on this topic. Also search the Family History Library Catalog for naturalization records available from the Salt Lake City library. This information could probably also be accessed at the Family History Center's website at familysearch.org.

Military Records

Current military records from WW II to the present are beyond the scope of this book. One group of early San Diego military records is in the archives at the San Diego Historical Society and this collection is described as follows:

> **Militia Rolls. 1853-1894. PRC, p. 25. Annual rolls show the names of all men eligible for local military service. After 1880, the records also indicate residence. There are several missing years. Arranged chronologically.**

The Family History Center has a group of records called "California Military Records/Pension List 1883" on Film No. 1,035,781, Item 3. This is a listing of veterans living in California who were pension recipients in 1883. This list may be a valuable resource to search for those with ancestors from other California counties as the records include pension recipients from all over the state for 1883. The list for San Diego County includes the following veterans, wives, or parents of the veterans:

California 1883 Military Pension List

No. of Certif	Name of Pensioner	P.O. Address	Reason for Pension	Monthly Rate	Date of Original Allowance
31,053	Willard Whitney	Bernardo	GSW in face	$5.00*	Feb 1877
13,177	Ed A. Foss	El Cajon	GSW l. leg	$2.00	Jan 1863
51,671	Eli T. Blackmer	National City	Chron. diarr	$3.50*	Oct 1865
131,772	Robt. E. Haywood	National City	GSW l. shoul	$4.00	Dec 1876
105,410	Jacob Bergman	Oak Grove	GSW l. shoul	$12.00*	Jan 1877
62,594	Levi H. Utt	Pala	Unstated	$20.00	Aug 1866
13,218	Chas. C. Watson	Poway	Loss rt arm	$24.00	Aug 1874
104,222	Delarau Craft	Poway	GSW rt thigh	$2.66*	Jul 1870
144,194	Chas. M. Burks	San Diego	GSW l. arm	$4.00	Mar 1877
33,213	Sampson Ward	San Diego	Wd face	$18.00	Not stated
180,451	Walter Parker	San Diego	Malaria	$18.00	Not stated
187,729	John F. Miles	San Diego	GSW l arm	$17.00	Apr 1881
39,301	Alexander Smith	San Diego	Frac patella	$4.00	Mar 1865
106,792	Hiram Harrell	San Diego	Wd l thigh	$2.00	Nov 1870
9,142	Hiram S. Hall	San Diego	Aneurism/aorta	$24.00	Not stated
159,622	John Allen	San Diego	Dis lungs	$18.00	May 1879
179,994	Wm. J. England	San Diego	Dis lungs	$18.00	Dec 1880
154,395	Henry V. Richil	San Diego	GSW r chest	$8.00	Jul 1878
68,150	Martin Hamilton	San Diego	Amput r arm	$24.00	Oct 1874
102,617	Albert Gore	San Diego	Chron. diarr	$17.00	Not stated
164,730	Martin Telleu	San Diego	Chron rheu	$12.00	Feb 1880
142,161	Maria Burton	San Diego	Widow	$30.00	Apr 1870
15,773	Eliz. Brewster	San Diego	Widow 1812	$8.00	Jan 1879
193,453	Lyman Roberts	San Diego	Father	$8.00	Oct 1881
123,591*	Curtis Johnson	San Dieguito	GSW l arm	$15.00	Jun 1873
218,208	Alfred Confer	Temecula	GSW l thigh	$6.00	Sep 1882

The San Diego Historical Society also has military records pertaining to Civil War veterans who migrated to San Diego after the war. These are in a set of six boxes at Call No. MS 365, "Military Records". The boxes contain Grand Army of the Republic (G.A.R.) intake records for the Heintzelman Post and Datus Coon Post of the G.A.R., which was an organization of Union veterans of the Civil War.

The G.A.R. intake records recorded details such as the veteran's name, age, birthplace or state, Civil War unit, length of service, when and where discharged, the year the veteran applied for admittance to the local posts, and the date when the veterans left the posts. This collection also includes Heintzelman Post address books, ledger books and minutes of meetings of the Heintzelman Post, which give insights into the operation of the post and its activities.

These intake records were transcribed by Barbara Palmer and are included in a book entitled *The Civil War Veterans of San Diego*, which documents nearly 2,000 Civil War veterans who migrated to San Diego after the war. The book also contains tombstone inscriptions and cemetery office records for nearly 1,000 of the Civil War veterans and for the wives of those who were married. The book is available at the California Room of the downtown San Diego Public Library, the San Diego Historical Society, the San Diego Genealogical Society Library and at the Family History Center. The book will be republished in 2005 by Willow Bend Books, a division of Heritage Books, Inc., web address www.WillowBendBooks.com.

In the Genealogy Room of the downtown San Diego Public Library is a book entitled *Records of California Men in the War of the Rebellion, 1861-1867*, by Brig.Gen. Richard H. Orton. This book documents the various infantry and calvary units (including native Hispanic units) that were assembled in the State of California during the time periods described in the title. J. Carlyle Parker has done an index to the Orton book entitled *"Personal Name Index to Orton's Records of California Men in the War of the Rebellion"* which is located in the Genealogy Room of the downtown San Diego Public Library.

The Family History Center has a group of records called "California Civil War Veteran Burial Listings" (Film No. 1,000,138, Item 4). This is a compilation of burial locations for many veterans who served in California volunteer units during the Civil War. Most of the burials being reported in this source occurred in the Los Angeles area. No veterans in this source were buried in San Diego.

The Family History Center has the "1890 Census of Union Veterans and Widows of Union Veterans of the Civil War" but be aware that the records of this special census for Alabama through Kansas and the first half of Kentucky were apparently lost in a fire. Thus California is not represented on this microfilm.

A major source for research on the Union forces of the Civil War (although it does contain much information on the Confederate forces as well) is Frederick H. Dyer's *A Compendium of the War of the Rebellion*, located in the History Reference area at the downtown San Diego Public Library. This work originally consisted of 4,025 typed sheets and when published contained three parts:

> Part 1: Summarizes enlistments and losses, all national cemeteries and their locations, and lists by state 2,494 regiments, 126 battalions and 939 batteries and independent companies. It also lists 900 Federal regiments that lost 50 or more men in combat, grouped by state and numbers killed and wounded. Additionally, it contains an alphabetical list of 7,800 persons who commanded brigades and larger organizations and all of the Union's departments, armies, corps, divisions and brigades.

> Part 2: Contains a record of all Civil War engagements and losses, arranged chronologically and by state. This listing comprises 10,455 military events.

> Part 3: Contains 3,550 Regimental Histories, including where each unit was organized, when it was mustered into the Federal service, the higher headquarters it was assigned to, the areas and actions where it served, changes in its designations and status, the date it was mustered out, and the numbers of those who died from battle causes or diseases.

The *Compendium* is a primary tool for researching both individual soldiers, the regiments in which they served, and the broader scope of the Civil War, its engagements and campaigns.

If you have an ancestor that was a Civil War veteran, you may want to obtain their service record and pension papers from the National Archives in Washington, D.C. You need to use a National Archives form to order such records, and to expedite matters you should have your veteran's pension file number.

There is a ring binder at the Family History Center containing an index entitled *United States Military Records--Pension Index File--1861-1934*, at Call No. "Ref - Military Records - Civil War." The index lists microfilms which <u>do not contain an individual veteran's pension record but do contain their pension file number</u>. These are arranged by the military units the veterans fought with during the war: "Union Troops," "Confederate Troops" or "Civil War Colored Troops" and the listings in this index read like the following:

Name	Film No.
Aab-Ackerman	540,757
Ackerman-Adams	540,758
Adams-Ahh	540,759

Say your veteran's last name was "Agee." His pension file number would appear on Film No. 540,759. So scan the lists in the ring binders for the microfilm that contains the alphabetical range appropriate for the name of the ancestor that you are researching. Once you obtain the microfilm number, see if that microfilm is currently available at your local Family History Center.

If the film is not in, then you must order that microfilm from the main branch of the Family History Center at Salt Lake City which you can do through your local Family History Center for a nominal charge. Once you obtain the microfilm which might contain your ancestor's pension file number, scan through the microfilm (the names are in alphabetical order) to obtain your Civil War veteran's pension file number. Be aware, however, that if your veteran's name is <u>missing from the microfilm it should be on</u>, then your ancestor or his wife might not have applied for or obtained a pension for service in the Civil War.

After obtaining your ancestor's pension file number, you can order copies of your veteran's pension file. Call the National Archives in Laguna Niguel at (949) 360-2611 and ask them to send you NAFT Form 80. (More information about the National Archives is given at the end of this book). Fill out the form and send it to the Washington, D.C. address on the form, <u>NOT the St. Louis address</u>. Include your ancestor's pension file number on this form.

The National Archives will send you an estimate of the cost to photocopy your ancestor's pension file, and to obtain the records faster, you may charge the cost to your credit card. The pension files contain a wide selection of records from explanations of a soldier's place of birth and details about his family through his Civil War experiences to his discharge, application for his pension and possible information about his death and burial location.

There is a book at the Family History Center and at the downtown San Diego Public Library entitled *Civil War Research Guide*, by Stephen McManus (published in 2003) which will be of help in searching your Civil War ancestor and in obtaining his pension records from the National Archives. Finally, the Family History Center publishes a number of "Research Outlines" on a variety of topics. A Military Records guide called *"Research Outline: U.S. Military Records"* is helpful in learning research sources for military records. The guide can be purchased from the Family History Center for a nominal charge.

Marriage Records
There are two lists of marriages of Hispanic couples performed by Catholic missionaries which are entitled *Marriages: Book I, Mission San Diego Register* (covering Catholic marriages for the years 1775 through the early 1880s) and *Marriages Small Book II, 1848-1858*, a marriage book possibly kept by Fr. Holbein which contains marriages for only 42 couples. These records are handwritten copies of original records, apparently, and they were made available by Georgia Callian of the Old Town Descendants group. They

are somewhat illegible but at least provide a list of marriages for the stated dates. Call Old Town San Diego State Historic Park for more information on the Old Town Descendants group at (619) 220-5420.

The above records list the date of marriage, the couple being married, the parents of the couple being married, and witnesses, where available. In some instances in Book I, the church where the couple was married is given with words describing the church as follows: "Church of the Royal Presidio", "Presidio", and "Church of the Mission". A notation for what appears to be September, 1836 states "Last for Church of Royal Presidio". The next notation possibly in November or December of 1836 is "Church of the Port". A listing in 1839 says "First Capilla del Puerto". After that, there are listings for "Church of Port" and "Chapel of the Port" and in 1846 a note reads "Chapel of the Port (Last Entry)". No church is mentioned in Book 1 after that date.

The old chapel on Presidio Hill was in ruins by 1836 and perhaps the notations for "Church of the Port" meant a room where church events took place which was known to have been established at the Estudillo House at Old Town. The "Chapel of the Port (Last Entry)" notation in 1846, however, is too early a date for marriages to have been discontinued at the Estudillo House because it is believed that church events occurred there until around 1858 when the Adobe Chapel was opened at Old Town. More research is needed to determine where the "Church", "Capilla" or "Chapel" of the Port were located.

The only mention of the location of marriages in Record Book II are the following: "Church of San Diego" (for a marriage in 1848), "Church of Pueblo" (for a marriage in 1850), "Sala of Bandini House" (for two marriages in 1851), and "Sala of Maria Antonia Alvarado Snook" (for a marriage in 1853). There are also five marriages at San Luis Rey in 1858 which are reported in this book.

Another set of records reflecting the marriages of Hispanic individuals is at the San Diego Historical Society and is called "Matrimonial Records--San Diego, California: 1776-1842" at Call No. 929.3/San. Please note, however, that the records only go to 1833, then two marriages were recorded in 1834, one in 1835 and one in 1842 for a grand total of 136 marriages. It is unknown whether some marriages were missing from the San Diego Historical Society document but for comparison the Old Town Descendant's list, discussed above, has 28 marriages recorded from 1834 to 1842, and many more after that.

The San Diego Historical Society records are typewritten, several in Spanish but most in English, and list the date of marriage, the couple being married, the parents of the couple being married, and witnesses, plus the names of the missionary priests that officiated at the marriages. The name of the church was given for most of these marriages as the "Mission Church" or "Presidio Church" (the last marriage there was in 1835). The marriage in 1842 was at the "Little Chapel of the Port of San Diego."

The missionary priests who officiated at these marriages are historical figures in their own right, and they included the following: Fr. Vicente Fuster (1776), then Indian marriages only in 1777, then Fr. Fermin Francisco de Lasuen (1778-1779), then Indian marriages only in 1780, then Fr. Lasuen (1781-1783) and Fr. Juan Figuer (1783), then Indian marriages only from 1784-1787, then Fr. Juan Mariner (1788), then Fr. Hilario Torrent (1789).

Then there were Indian marriages only in 1790, then Fr. Torrent (1791-1795), Indian marriages only in 1796, then Fr. Pedro Esteban (1797) and Fr. Juan Mariner (1797), then Indian marriages only in 1798, then Fr. Mariner (1799). Then Indian marriages only in 1800 and 1801, then Fr. Josef Barona or Varona (1802), then Indian marriages only in 1803, then Fr. Barona adds marriages he conducted (1798 to 1804) into the record. Then marriages up to 1814 were conducted by Fr. Mariano Paycras (1805), Fr. Josef Sanchez (1805-1806, 1809-1810, 1812 and 1815-1818), Fr. Nicholas Lazaros (1807), Fr. Barona (1807 and 1809-1810), then Fr. Jose Garcia (1808) and Fr. Pedro Panto in 1811-1812). Note that there were Indian marriages only in 1813, 1819 and 1820.

Besides two marriages, one conducted by Fr. Felix Caballero (1824) and one conducted by Fr. Antonio Menendez (1829), the remaining marriages from 1814 to 1842 were conducted either by Fr. Fernando Martin (in 1814, 1816-1817, 1821-1823, 1828, 1830-1835) or Fr. Vicente Pasqual Oliva (1821-1822, 1824, 1825-1827, 1829-1832 and 1842). In fact, Fr. Oliva was the last Franciscan Missionary at Mission San Diego de Alcala and he left when American forces took up residence at the mission in 1846.

For more information on original mission marriage records, contact Janet Bartel at the Mission San Diego de Alcala (619) 283-7319. For recent marriages contact the church archives at (619) 490-8208.

Another book for sale at the San Diego Genealogical Society, *Episcopal Church Records--Holy Trinity Episcopal and St. Pauls Episcopal* contains a listing of marriages from April, 1873 to June, 1887. An example of one of the marriage records in this book is the following:

> Remondino, Peter C. & Earle, Sophie, at res. of Mr. Earle. 27 Sep 1877. Wit: Father & brother of bride and B. Etcheverry. [Note: an earlier citation read: Etcheverry, Bernard & Earle, Louise at home of Mr. Earle. 2 Apr 1877.] Minister: Rev. Hobart Chetwood.

See also Ben Dixon's book *San Diego's Religious Heritage* and William Smythe's *History of San Diego* at the downtown San Diego Public Library to determine when the older churches of San Diego were started. If those churches still exist, they will have marriage records.

Marriage records are available at the County of San Diego from the early 1850s. "Public marriage records" are those which are open to the public and are available for viewing and for purchase in Room 260 of the County Administration Building. "Confidential marriage records" began at the county in 1973, are not open to the public, and may be viewed and purchased only by the bride or groom, who must show identification.

Indexes to marriage records at the county also cannot be accessed by the public. The county has indexes to marriage records on microfiche from 1904 to 1972. Marriage records before then are in old fragile books which are not available for public viewing. The old books were arranged either by the name of the groom or the bride. The first groom's and brides books give an idea of the year when grooms and brides names began appearing in the first books for various letters of the alphabet. For example, groom surnames starting with the letter "A" were indexed from 1850 on because grooms with surnames beginning with "A" were arriving at the County to apply for marriage licenses. But grooms with surnames beginning with the letter "L" did not start appearing in the old books until 1859, as seen on the chart below.

Grooms	Brides	Grooms	Brides
A: 1850 on	1850 on	N: 1874 on	1867 on
B: 1858 on	1859 on	O: 1859 on	1859 on
C: 1859 on	1859 on	P: 1850 on	1856 on
D: 1851 on	1859 on	Q: 1876 on	1872 on
E: 1857 on	1860 on	R: 1859 on	1859 on
F: 1854 on	1854 on	S: 1859 on	1859 on
G: 1859 on	1857 on	T: 1864 on	1869 on
H: 1856 on	1860 on	U: 1876 on	1867 on
I: 1872 on	1882 on	V: 1866 on	1859 on
J: 1851 on	1859 on	W: 1857 on	1857 on
K: 1864 on	1858 on	X: None	None
L: 1859 on	1859 on	Y: 1877 on	1850 on
M: 1859 on	1850 on	Z: 1874 on	1882 on
Mc: 1865 on	1862 on		

Early marriages are also listed in a San Diego Genealogical Society publication for sale entitled *Newspaper Records: Vital Statistics from San Diego Newspapers: 1851-1885.* This book contains marriage notices in the *San Diego Herald* from August 24, 1853 to November 12, 1858 and from marriage notices in the *San Diego Union* from November 1, 1868 to January 14, 1885. The book is fully indexed.

Early marriage records are also available at the San Diego Historical Society and they include the following records from the County Recorder's Office:

> **Marriage Certificates. 1880-1881. PRC, p. 37. Certificates show the names of bride, groom, and witnesses; name and title of person officiating; nativity of bride, groom, and parents; and dates of marriage and recording. Arranged chronologically and indexed by name.**
>
> **Quarterly Returns of Marriages and Births. 1858-1860. PRC, p. 38. Returns of marriage show names, age, color, residence, and nativity for bride and groom; date and location of marriage; name, residence, and position of person officiating; and date of recording. Arranged chronologically and indexed by name.**

The California Room of the downtown San Diego Public Library has a microfiche listing of marriage records from 1960 to 1986 for the entire state of California.

Divorce Records

Divorce records are found in the Superior Court Older Records office at 220 Broadway, San Diego, Ph: (619) 531-3244. Divorce records before 1960 are not indexed and are in old ledger books covering ten year time periods. The 1940-1949 book had names filed by letter of the alphabet and then chronologically, and divorce records were mixed in with civil case filings. When searching the "H" surnames recently, it was also found that listings in the 1940-1949 ledger book would run from 1940-1949 for a few pages and then start over with 1940 and go to 1949 again within the same letter of the alphabet. Thus research in divorce records before 1960 could prove to be a tedious process unless the exact date the divorce was filed is known.

Occupational Records

Some occupational records are memorialized in books about particular occupations. One of the best of these is *San Diego's Legal Lore and the Bar*, which describes the founding of the San Diego County Bar and the judges and attorneys that made up this group. This book has biographies of judges who served in San Diego, including Benjamin Hayes, Oliver Witherby, Edwin Parker, Norman Conklin, and David Hoffman. This book is available at the downtown San Diego Public Library. See also the listing for the San Diego County Public Law Library, above, for more information on the holdings of that library.

The San Diego County Medical Society was founded before 1900 and has old index cards on file with information on early and more recent doctors of San Diego who applied for membership in this organization. The County Medical Society also published a journal from the 1920s on which contains much information about and photos of doctors. Early applications to the County Medical Society are on file in the Special Collections Department at San Diego State University.

There are books on San Diego architects at the downtown San Diego Public Library such as Bruce Kamerling's book on Irving Gill and another book entitled *Five California Architects*. There are theses on local architects (William Hebbard, Edward Quale, the Reid Brothers, Richard Requa, Lillian Rice and Hazel Waterman) and the location of these theses was discussed above in "Theses About Prominent People."

There are books and articles on merchants like George Marston and builders like Roscoe Hazard. Elizabeth MacPhail's book, *The Influence of German Immigrants on the Growth of San Diego*, discusses the occupations of a number of people discussed in her book. Check the subject catalog at libraries around San Diego to see if there is a book or some reference to individuals with various occupations.

Census Records
The Family History Center has San Diego census records <u>printed in book form</u> for the years 1850 to 1880. Soundex indexes for California for 1880, 1900 and 1910 are also available at the Family History Center, as are Enumeration District microfilms for California for 1900, 1910, and 1920. The 1910 Enumeration District information is also available on microfiche. Printed census books for the Federal Census of 1850, 1860 and 1870 and for the State Census of 1852 are for sale by the San Diego Genealogical Society.

Census records <u>printed in book form</u> at the California Room of the downtown San Diego Public Library include the 1850 California Census, the 1850 Federal Census for San Diego and the 1870 Census for San Diego County. The downtown San Diego Public Library also has San Diego County census records on microfilm from 1850 to 1920 in the Newspaper Room. Additionally, the 1860 California Census Index is on eight microfiche in both the California Room and the Genealogy Room.

The Genealogy Room of the downtown San Diego Public Library also has *San Diego County, California: Index to the 1900 Census* at Call No. 929.3794/SAN, which was compiled by the North County Genealogical Society. The San Diego Genealogical Society Library and the Carlsbad Library may also have a copy of this index. The index contains an alphabetical listing of heads of households and any other surnames found within the house, and the citations read like the following:

Name	**Enumeration District/Page**
Abbey, Eunice	202-1
Abbott, Mrs. E.	197-6

The authors explain that the San Diego County Census for 1900 is on two rolls of microfilm prepared by the National Archives and Records Service. Roll T623-99 includes Enumeration Districts 172 through 199, and Sheets 1-4 of Enumeration District 200. Roll T623-100 continues the rest of the census for the county. Fort Rosecrans is not assigned an Enumeration District number, and appears in the index as "Fort Rosecrans." At the time of the 1900 census, San Diego County included what is now Imperial County. This 1900 census index is invaluable for helping to locate the Enumeration District for individuals being researched. Once the Enumeration District is identified, you can more easily find the individual on the microfilm containing the 1900 census at the Family History Center.

The San Diego Historical Society has the following:

> **U.S. Census--Manuscript. 1850, 1860, 1870, 1880, 1900, 1910. PRC, p. 63. Transcripts of decentennial census schedules may include the following information for San Diego County individuals: name, age, sex, color, occupation, value of real and personal property, place of birth, marital status, and education. Schedules for 1880, 1900 and 1910 on microfilm only.**

Finally, the Family History Center has census records on microfilm for all states and all years.

Voter Registers
The Great Register of Voters generally shows the name of the person registering to vote and their age, nativity, occupation, local residence, whether naturalized, and date the person registered to vote. Volumes after 1892 also indicate height, complexion, color of eyes and hair, visible marks and scars, and post office address. The entries are arranged alphabetically by name of voter.

The downtown San Diego Public Library has the Great Register of Voters for selected years from 1866 through 1909. The Family History Center has the Great Register of Voters from 1866-1873, 1866-1879, and 1880-1887. The San Diego Genealogical Society has a publication for sale entitled *Great Register of Voters, San Diego County: 1866-1879*. The San Diego Historical Society has the Great Register of

Voters for selected years from 1877-1898. The Historical Society also has the following group of records:

> **Registrations. 1902, 1906. PRC, p. 34. Record indexes the Great Register of San Diego County, listing name, address, and age of voters in city and outside precincts. Arranged alphabetically by name of voter.**

The Great Register of Voters has also been published for the entire state of California for 1890, and thus one can see the spread of individuals with similar surnames across the state. The Family History Center may have a copy of this Great Register on CD/ROM. The Genealogy Room of the downtown San Diego Public Library has a copy at Call No. 929.37946/SAN and an index is at Call No. 929.3794/California.

The ease of use of the Great Register makes it a valuable tool for genealogical purposes. Alphabetical listings such as this allow you to determine if others of the same surname were also in San Diego. Follow up research in the Great Register with information from the census and other sources to fully establish that your ancestor was indeed in San Diego at an early date.

City Directories

City directories are a quick way to place individuals in San Diego from the late 1880s on. The San Diego Historical Society has several early directories, then the Pacific Coast Directories of 1882-1885 and finally City Directories from 1886-1984. There are printed City Directories at the California Room of the downtown San Diego Public Library from the late 1880s to 1984. The Newspaper Room also has City Directories from 1886-1950 on 25 reels of microfilm. The Family History Center has City Directories for the years 1924, 1926, 1940, and 1958-1974. There are also City Directories for sale on the third floor of Wahrenbrocks Book Store in downtown San Diego.

Early City Directories listed wives, wives as widows, occupations, and deaths of individuals. An example of the latter from the City Directory for 1911 is: "Dr. Gilbert P. Bennett died 10/19/1910, aged 75". Earlier City Directories listed San Diego proper and then separate lists for outlying areas like La Mesa, Coronado and National City, which make them a little more difficult to research. Reverse directories appeared within City Directories from 1926 on and listed the streets of San Diego and who lived at various addresses along those streets. Scan the City Directories to see when an individual is first listed and when they dropped out of the directories. Check movement around the city by noting an individual's various addresses, and also check the reverse directories to see if people with similar surnames are listed on a street.

Newspapers

One of the best sources at the downtown San Diego Public Library's Newspaper Room is the collection of newspapers on microfilm and the fact that there are enough reader/printers to spend time researching and making copies of obituaries and other items of interest. The most important microfilm holdings in the Newspaper Room are the following, listed in the order in which the newspapers were created:

> **San Diego Herald:** 1851-1860 (incomplete)
> **San Diego Union:** October 10, 1868-February 1, 1992
> **San Diego Sun:** July 1881-November 1939 (Incomplete)
> **San Diego Evening Tribune:** December 1895-February 1, 1992
> **San Diego Union-Tribune:** February 2, 1992 to the present

The California Room at the downtown San Diego Public Library has an index on microfiche to individuals, organizations, obituaries, and events which were discussed in these early newspapers. The newspapers were not indexed from 1904 to 1926 but do cover the time periods of 1851 to 1903 and from 1930 to 1983. The index is invaluable in shortening the length of time necessary to find articles about your ancestor if they appeared in the newspaper for some reason and if the article about them was indexed.

Find a citation in this index to a newspaper article about a subject, individual, organization or event that you are interested in and then go next door to the Newspaper Room to view the newspaper on microfilm for the year and date you need. Be aware that at times an article will appear in a newspaper other than the *San Diego Union*, for example, and if it does the index cards will note that fact. If you don't realize this, you will find yourself viewing a *San Diego Union* newspaper microfilm for the date in question but in reality you need to view the microfilm for the *San Diego Herald*.

Even if you don't find an obituary in these indexes, if you know the approximate date of death of your ancestor, just scan the "Obituaries" portion of the *San Diego Union* on microfilm for dates about five days after the date of death to see if there is an obituary for your ancestor.

The San Diego Genealogical Society has for sale the book *Newspaper Records: Vital Records From San Diego Newspapers: 1851-1875* which really makes life easier because the index is in print. The book contains several pages of births (1854-1859), marriages (1853-1858) and deaths (1851-1856) from the *San Diego Herald* and about 80 pages of vital records from the *San Diego Union* for 1868-1885. The book can also be found at the Family History Center and at the Genealogy Room of the downtown San Diego Public Library. Make notes from this book about the newspapers you wish to access, and then look at the various articles, obituaries, etc. on the newspaper microfilms at the downtown San Diego Public Library.

The San Diego Historical Society has a 70+ page printout of all of its newspaper holdings. It has the same microfiche index to newspapers as the San Diego Public Library does, but only one film reader. Contact the Historical Society at (619) 232-6203, ext. 123 or 124 for more information on the Newspaper collection.

Church Registers
The San Diego Genealogical Society has for sale a book entitled *Episcopal Church Records: Holy Trinity Episcopal and St. Pauls Episcopal*. This publication contains records for Holy Trinity Church, a church in existence from 1872-1886 which became St. Pauls Episcopal on January 22, 1887. The publication contains the following: a Holy Trinity list of parishioners for 1872, a list of 194 baptisms from 1872 to 1887, a list of 82 marriages from 1873 to 1887, a list of 89 burials from 1873 to 1887, a list of 189 communicants from 1872 to 1883, and a list of 788 communicants of St. Pauls on Easter Day, 1887. The old St. Pauls Episcopal Church is now St. Pauls Episcopal Cathedral, located in the Bankers Hill area of San Diego.

Another San Diego Genealogical Society publication contains records of members of First Presbyterian Church on Date Street in downtown San Diego. This book is indexed and contains some records from the late 1800s, but the majority of the individuals listed were members of this church from 1900 on. See also Ben Dixon's book *San Diego's Religious Heritage* and William Smythe's book *History of San. Diego* at the downtown San Diego Public Library to determine when the older churches of San Diego were started. If those churches still exist, they will have baptismal, marriage and burial records.

Property Records
Property records have been compiled by the County of San Diego since 1850. These records are in Room 130 of the County Assessor's Office at the County Administration Building, 1600 Pacific Highway in San Diego. The earliest grantor/grantee indexes at the County are on microfilm and are very difficult to read. The grantor/grantee indexes are alphabetical by surname and give the deed book and page upon which the particular deeds that you are researching appear. You must then go to microfilms which contain those deed books to view the deeds. Property records can be printed out from reader/printers at $2 per page.

Alpha and numeric property indexes from 1982 to the present and an alpha index from 1970 to 1989 are on the computer at the County, and can also be accessed online at www.sdarcc.com.

Because the early property records on microfilm are so difficult to read, a publication for sale by the San Diego Genealogical Society takes on greater importance. This publication, called *Land Records For San*

Diego County: Grantor Index To Deed Books A-E and 1-25, contains an alphabetical listing of grantors in each of the deed books which were transcribed, shows who the grantors sold property to, the dates of recordation of the deeds, and the deed book and page upon which the deeds appear.

Having this book saves a lot of time for those researching early deeds because you can make notations at home of the deeds you wish to research and then go directly to the deed microfilms to view the deeds. The book also shows who was involved in the earliest property transfers in San Diego. A copy of this book is at the California Room of the downtown San Diego Public Library and also at the Family History Center.

The San Diego Historical Society has the following information on deeds from the County Recorder:

> **Index to Deeds. 1850-1886. PRC, p. 37. Index shows names of grantors and grantees, date of deed, and book and page of recording. Arranged alphabetically by name of grantor and grantee.**
>
> **Deeds, Miscellaneous. 1850-1919. PRC, p. 37. Deed instruments show names of grantor and grantee, a legal description of property, amount of consideration, book and page of recording, and date filed. Arranged chronologically by date of filing and indexed alphabetically by names of grantor and grantee.**

Additionally, the Historical Society has the following from the City Clerk's Office:

> **Deeds (Deed Record). 1850-1947. PRC, p. 21. Transcripts of legal deeds showing real property and property rights obtained by the City of San Diego. Entries include the date and type of deed, location, names of owners, amounts of compensation paid, and purpose of city acquisition. Arranged chronologically by date of deed.**

One research tool which appeared in Dennis Sharp's "A Guide to the San Diego Historical Society Public Records Collection: 2001 Edition, Revised, Updated and Edited" are city lot books, which are available for research purposes at the San Diego Historical Society. The date range of the lot books is from 1890 to 1930.

The lot books contain yearly property assessments, the property owner's name, acreage, value of improvements, and mortgage number. Anyone researching property should look at the lot books when conducting property research for the years from 1890 to 1930.

Tax Records

San Diego County has tax and assessment records dating from the beginning of the county in 1850 which are available at Room 103 of the County Administration Building, Room 103, 1600 Pacific Highway, San Diego. For property records information, call (619) 236-3771. The San Diego Genealogical Society has two books for sale involving tax records and they are: *Taxpayers, San Diego County, 1850-1852* and *Tax Assessment Rolls for San Diego County, 1853-1863*. The San Diego Genealogical Society also has for sale the Federal Census of 1860, which has a section on land and improvements owned by individuals and the tax being being assessed on the property.

The San Diego Historical Society has the following records from the County Assessor's Office:

> **Assessment Lists. 1853-1873. PRC, p. 25. List of property, real and personal, show name of property owner, legal description of property, nature and value of taxable personal property (farm animals, financial instruments, etc.) and date filed. Arranged chronologically and indexed by name of property owner.**

Reports of the County Assessor. 1875-1894. PRC, p. 25. Annual summaries of county taxable property--real and personal--show description of property or item, values, and totals. Arranged chronologically.

Assessment Roll (Tax Book). 1850-1854, 1859, 1869, 1871-1876. PRC, p. 26. Rolls of real property and secured personal property show owner's name, residence, legal description of property, number of acres, value of property and improvements, value of personal property, total taxes due, and date paid. Arranged alphabetically by name of taxpayer.

The Family History Center has a publication entitled *Taxpayers of San Diego County, Book II--1851*. This book lists tax assessment rolls for the early 1850s but represents only a partial list because most of the entries are for ranches with only a few taxpayers listed from San Diego proper.

Civil and Criminal Records

The San Diego Superior Court civil and criminal records are available for viewing in Older Records at 220 Broadway, San Diego, CA 92101. Records before 1960 are not indexed and are in old ledger books divided into ten year periods. Contact Older Records at (619) 531-3244 for additional information about these files.

The San Diego Historical Society has the following Civil/Criminal case files:

County Court Case Files--Civil and Criminal. 1850-1880. PRC, p. 49. Case files contain the official documents of the court including complaint, subpoenas, arrest warrants, transcripts of testimony, jury verdicts, court actions and judgments. Arranged chronologically by court date and indexed by names of plaintiffs and defendants, and cause.

Court of Sessions Case Files--Civil and Criminal. 1850-1860. PRC, p. 50. Case files contain the official documents of the court including complaint, subpoenas, arrest warrants, transcripts of testimony, jury verdicts, court actions and judgments. Arranged chronologically by court date and indexed by names of plaintiffs, defendants, and cause.

District Court Case Files--Civil and Criminal. 1850-1880. PRC, p. 50. Case files of civil and criminal proceedings show names of plaintiffs, defendants, and judge; court dates and actions. Papers contained in typical case files include: complaints, subpoenas, affidavits of witnesses, receipts, arrest warrants, testimony, verdicts, and other documents. Arranged numerically by case number and indexed by names of plaintiffs and defendants.

Grand Jury Reports. 1906-1928. PRC, p. 51. Record contains official transcripts of preliminary and final reports of investigations conducted in San Diego County, including supplemental reports and audits of county departments. Arranged chronologically by year.

Justice Court Case Files--Civil and Criminal. 1870-1918. PRC, p. 52. Justice court case files show names of plaintiff, defendant, and justice; court dates and actions. Papers contained in the files may include: complaint, subpoena, affidavits of witnesses, receipts, arrest warrants, verdict, and testimony. Arranged alphabetically by name of township and chronologically thereunder by court date. Indexed by names of plaintiff and defendant, subject, and township.

Superior Court Case Files--Civil and Criminal. 1879-1921. PRC, p. 58. Case files contain the official documents of the court including complaint, subpoenas, arrest warrants, transcripts of testimony, jury verdicts, court actions, and judgments. Arranged chronologically.

Superior Court Judgements--Civil. 1886-1947. PRC, p. 59. Judgment books show the case number; names of plaintiffs, defendants, and judge; and all judgments and orders. Arranged chronologically by date of judgment and indexed (vols. 19-119) by name of plaintiff.

Hospital Records

The San Diego Genealogical Society has published in its *Leaves & Saplings* magazine the early records from the old County hospital and poor farm in Mission Valley, the forerunner of the county hospital in Hillcrest which is now UCSD Medical Center. These records date from the early 1870s and there are some county hospital records from the 1920s. The records include a category for race and also note the residence of the patients and whether the patient died in the hospital or was discharged.

These records can be compared with Mount Hope Cemetery records, the city cemetery which opened for burials in 1869, or with records for the two Catholic cemeteries at the time--El Campo Santo Cemetery in Old Town and Calvary Cemetery in Mission Hills--to determine where the individuals who died in the hospital were buried and more about them from tombstone inscriptions and cemetery office records. (See more about cemeteries and their records below.)

A hospital still in operation which had old records is Mercy Hospital in Hillcrest. The forerunner of this hospital was St. Joseph's Hospital, located at 6th and University in Hillcrest. St. Joseph's Hospital was started by the Sisters of Mercy in 1881-2, and the hospital moved to its present location and became "Mercy Hospital" in the early 1920s. This hospital was recently acquired by Scripps Hospital.

St. Joseph's Hospital started admitting patients around 1882, and copies of the early records of this hospital are at the San Diego Historical Society and the San Diego Genealogical Society. One historical figure who died at St. Joseph's Hospital was Fr. Antonio Ubach, the priest in charge of the San Diego Catholic diocese from 1866 until his death in 1907.

The above hospitals are the two oldest hospitals in the city. There were some small hospitals in downtown San Diego from the 1870s to the 1920s, but records for those probably do not exist. If you are trying to research hospital records and the hospital you need information from is still in existence, contact the hospital to determine if they have old records. Records may or may not be available, however, depending on their record retention schedules.

Death/Burial Records

Records concerning the death and burial of individuals in San Diego are among the largest collection of records available locally and include death certificates, probate records, coroner and mortuary records, and records of burials.

The earliest burial records available are for Mission San Diego de Alcala, Presidio Hill, and for El Campo Santo Cemetery in Old Town, and they are in the R. Clinton Griffin Collection of Catholic burial records. This collection represents records of burials for all of the earliest cemeteries in San Diego except for Holy Cross Cemetery, which is still in operation. The collection includes the following:

Mission Basilica San Diego De Alcala: Burials for Mission & Presidio, 1775-1831

El Campo Santo Cemetery [The Holy Field] San Diego, California: Burials 1849-1880

Mission San Diego de Alcala: Mission Hills Catholic Cemetery (Old Calvary): 1875-1969

Copies of these books are available at the San Diego Historical Society and may be available at the El Cajon Family History Center, 1270 So. Orange Avenue, El Cajon, CA. Phone: (619) 588-1426.

It must be noted that the book containing burials for Mission San Diego de Alcala and Presidio Hill has large gaps in the record numbers for burials. For example, Burial Nos. 1-3 are presented followed by Burial No. 5, then 10-11, then 13-21, then 25, then 38, then 50, then 114, then 118, etc. This may mean that more than one burial book was being kept by the early missionaries, and the second burial book has since been lost or is being kept at another location.

The Mission San Diego de Alcala and Presidio Hill burial book first lists the burials of Fr. Luis Jaume, Josef Manuel Arroyo and Josef Urselino, who were killed in an Indian raid and fire at Mission San Diego de Alcala in November, 1775. The book also has some Indian burials but mostly has burials of Hispanic soldiers and settlers and their wives and children. Of these, 73 Hispanic adults were buried on Presidio Hill, including the following important historical figures:

> Guillermo Carrillo, Jose Raymundo Carrillo and Alejo Antonio Gonzales of the 1769 Expedition to found California; important Presidio Hill figures like Juan Pablo Grijalva, Juan Francisco Lopez, and Petra Romero-Garcia, Maria del Rosario Marquez and two Romero children, the mother, wife and children of blacksmith Felipe Romero (who witnessed the 1775 Indian raid); and Cristobal Dominguez, Jose Maria Estudillo, Jose Manuel Machado, Francisco Serrano, Jose Miguel Silvas and Joseph Manuel Silvas, whose descendants were important to Old Town San Diego history.

Burials on Presidio Hill also included American Henry Delano Fitch, his daughter Natalia Fitch, and Englishman Joseph Snook. (See p. 16 of this book for more about these individuals).

The County of San Diego has a document entitled *Book of the Dead [Book A-1] of the Vicinity of San Diego, 1879: Transcribed and Translated from Mission San Diego Records by Ann W. Guern and Winifred Davidson, 1932-1933: Burials from 1849 to 1880 in Campo Santo (in Old Town--Old Spanish Cemetery)* which covers the same burials as the R. Clinton Griffin book does for this cemetery, but at times gives more details about these burials.

There is also a set of burial records compiled by Peter O'Malley, who was the caretaker for Calvary Cemetery near Grant School in Mission Hills. Copies of these records are at the San Diego Historical Society and the San Diego Genealogical Society, and they span a date range of 1897 to 1932. They are in four books:

> A book of cemetery records with the word "Record" on the front cover which includes burials from the late 1800s to around 1930.

> A book of cemetery records with the words "ROYAL Memorandum Book Trademark, Pat. Jan. 21, 1890" on the front cover which includes burials from 1913 to 1917.

> A book of cemetery records with the word "Composition" on the front cover which includes burials by various funeral homes from 1918 to 1919, with a few burials in the early 1920s.

> A book of cemetery records with the word "Exercises" on the front cover which includes burials from approximately 1918 to December, 1932.

The San Diego Historical Society has a copy of a map of Calvary Cemetery which was drawn when the cemetery was being grassed over and made into a passive recreation park. It contains many of the burials that took place there, but no one knows for certain how many individuals are buried at Calvary. Another map of Calvary Cemetery may be at the offices of Mount Hope Cemetery, as both Calvary and Mount Hope are operated by the City of San Diego. (See more about these two cemeteries under their respective listings below). Calvary Cemetery also has a memorial plaque listing names of individuals buried at this cemetery, but again, it is probably not a complete listing of all who are buried there.

The San Diego Genealogical Society has the book *Newspaper Records: Vital Statistics From San Diego Newspapers: 1851-1885* which contains death notices from the *San Diego Herald* from June, 1851 to March, 1859 and 80 pages of death notices and other vital records from the *San Diego Union* for 1868-1885. This book is fully indexed.

Death certificates (a few from 1849 on) are available in Room 260 of the County Administration Building, 1600 Pacific Highway in San Diego. Phone: (619) 237-0502. Anyone may view and/or purchase copies of death certificates. San Diego County has an index of death certificates from 1905 on a computerized system and also old index books containing death certificates from 1850 to 1904, but these indexes are no longer available for public inspection. Information in the older death index books is grouped alphabetically and then chronologically as individuals died.

As with marriage records, the dates at which the recording of death certificates began in the first death index book vary by letter of the alphabet. For example, if the surname you are researching starts with the letter "D", deaths certificates were recorded with surnames beginning with the letter "D" from 1851, but entries for the letter "K" were first recorded from 1871 on, so there is a great deal of variation in the first death index, as seen below:

A--Deaths from 1849 on	N--1852 on
B--1854 on	O--1851 on
C--1850 on	P--1850 on
D--1851 on	Q--1870 on
E--1851 on	R--1850 on
F--1863 on	S--1852 on
G--1853 on	T--1868 on
H--1868 on	U--1880 on
I--1854 on	V--1854 on
J--1853 on	W--1853 on
K--1871 on	X--None
L--1850 on	Y--1851 on
M--1851 on	Z--1851 on
Mc-1890 on	

The old ledger books have the following information: date of death, name of decedent, race, age at death, sex, marital status, nativity, cause of death, coroner or doctor attending, and occupation. Thus there is a good deal of information in these books, and the information on nativity is particularly useful to determine where your ancestor was born.

Most of the information in these books appears on the death certificate when you purchase it, but it is so much more interesting to see the old ledger books to determine if there is any more information available on your ancestor that does not appear on the death certificates.

The San Diego Historical Society has the following death records from the County Recorder and from a private collection:

Certificate of Death. 1873-1876. PRC, p. 37. Death certificates show the name, age, marital status, sex, occupation, and birthplace of deceased; names of medical attendant, person making report, and undertaker; location of burial; location, date and cause of death. Arranged chronologically by date of death and indexed by name.

The Family History Center has a valuable index entitled the "California Death Index, 1905-1929 and 1930-1939", Film No.s 1,686,044 through 1,686,048 for the earlier years, and Film No.s 1,686,048 through 1,686,050 for the later years. This is a compilation of death records from the State of California Department of Public Health, Bureau of Vital Statistics.

Information on this index is listed alphabetically by name of decedent, initials of spouse, age at death, county where the death was filed, date of death, and a number such as the following: 19-030543. The "19" stands for 1919, the year the death certificate was filed in the county of death; the "030543" is the state number under which the decedent's record is filed. Original death certificates are on file at the Office of the State Registrar of Vital Statistics. Copies of the death certificates are on file at the County Recorder's office in the county of death. Note: while these state records start in 1905, death records maintained by San Diego County started in the 1850s.

The California Room of the downtown San Diego Public Library has a death index on microfiche for the entire state of California from 1940 to 1995. As with all death records, once you have the date of death, you can look for an obituary of your ancestor in the newspaper microfilms at the Newspaper Room of the downtown San Diego Public Library.

You can also obtain information on deaths in California by accessing rootsweb on the Internet and clicking on California Death Records, or simply type "California Death Records" into Google or another search engine. Always, however, look for rootsweb listings for there is no charge for accessing rootsweb records. Or type "Social Security Death Index" into Google or another search engine to find individuals who were receiving Social Security benefits but who have died. Again, rootsweb may be one provider of this listing.

Probate Records/Wills
Probate records are at the "Older Records" office of the County of San Diego, located at 222 Broadway in downtown San Diego. Ph: (619) 531-3244. The records start in 1850 and go to a recent cutoff date. After that, the records are kept in the "Newer Records" area in the Hall of Justice, next door to 222 Broadway. Be aware that old probate ledger books must be searched, for an index to probate records is not available for probates filed before 1960. The ledger books are arranged by letter of the alphabet and chronologically as probates were filed.

The San Diego Historical Society has completed their cataloging of old probate court records from 1850 to 1908 and a list of the probates included in their files is available. The probate court files contain original wills, letters in both English and Spanish, court papers, inventories of estate property, genealogical information, and the final distribution of property, and some probates extend over a number of years.

Many individuals important to San Diego history are represented in the probate files, including Jose Antonio Aguirre, Jose Maria Alvarado, Frank Ames, Santiago E. Arguello, Cave Couts, Jose Antonio Estudillo, Maria Victoria Dominguez de Estudillo, Henry Delano Fitch, Francis Hinton, Richard Kerran.

Also, Bonifacio Lopez, Andrew Lyons, Jacob Mannasse, Moses Mannasse, Juan Maria Marron, George Phillips Marston, Patrick O'Neill, Juan Maria Osuna, Maria Antonia de Pedrorena, George Pendleton, Jose Antonio Pico (the brother of Pio and Andres Pico), Albert B. Smith, Lorenzo Soto, and Charles Taggart.

Additionally, the following probate records and wills are available at San Diego Historical Society:

> **Superior Court Probate Court Case Files. 1891-1920. PRC, p. 60. Case files contain vouchers, dispositions, and bills submitted to estates by creditors. Court testimony is found in some files. Arranged chronologically by year and indexed by name of estate.**

> **Superior Court Probate Orders and Decrees. 1886-1940. PRC, p. 60. Record contains court minutes, orders, and decrees showing name of estate, case number, and date of hearing; names of testator; attorneys, judge, witnesses, and legatees. Arranged chronologically by court date and indexed by name of estate.**

Superior Court Record of Wills. 1880-1927. PRC, p. 60. Record of wills probated in San Diego shows names of deceased (testator), heirs, and witnesses; dates of death and recording of will; and transcript of will. Arranged chronologically by recording date and indexed by name of testator.

Office of the Treasurer Estates of Deceased Persons. 1876-1886, 1923-1924. PRC, p. 42. Record of receipt and disposition of monies from estates shows name of deceased, date of entry, source and amount of receipts, date of disbursements and to whom disbursed, and names of heirs. Arranged chronologically by date of entry and partially indexed by name of deceased.

The Family History Center has a "Probate Index 1850-1922" and in it is written: "All information contained in these books was taken from the index of the San Diego County Superior Court Probate Records, located in the San Diego County Clerk's Office, Third Floor" and cover dates from July 1, 1850 to January 14, 1922. The listings are alphabetical, followed by the Probate Court file number assigned to the case. In some instances, guardianships for those who were incompetent and for minors are also reported.

Coroner Records

At the San Diego Historical Society, there is a group of records from the San Diego County Clerk entitled:

Coroner's Inquest Papers, 1853-1904. PRC, p. 33. Coroner's jury papers contain transcripts of testimony from inquests and certificates of death. Certificates show name, age, occupation, marital status, place of birth, length of residence in San Diego County, and previous residence of deceased; and date, cause, and location of death. Arranged chronologically by date of death and indexed by name, cause, and location.

The San Diego Genealogical Society has also published a book entitled *Coroner's Inquests of San Diego County 1871-1896*. In the volume it is stated: "This record dates from 4/18/1871 to 1/5/1896 and contains the name of the deceased, date of death and location, age at death, nativity, and occupation, where available, the names of coroner, witnesses, and jurors who heard the case, and a case number citation."

Mortuary Records

The San Diego Genealogical Society, in *Leaves & Saplings*, Vol. 27, No. 1, Jan-Mar 1999, published a list of old mortuaries in San Diego from 1869 to 1920 and they were the following. (Note: The mortuaries which started in the mid-1880s were in existence to serve those who migrated to San Diego during the boom years caused by the coming of the railroad to San Diego):

Johnson & Company (1869-1900), Johnson & Connell (1901-1911), Johnson Connell & Saum (1912-1915), Johnson - Saum Co. (1916-1920). This mortuary was located in downtown San Diego at two locations: 7th and D from 1869 until 1915, and 4th & Ash from 1916-1920. (more about this mortuary below).

John N. Young, (1886-1887), 5th near F, downtown San Diego.
Gallager & Schubel, (1886-1888), 657 4th, downtown San Diego.
Archer & Witherby, (1887-1888), 755 5th, downtown San Diego.
Breese & Byers, (1887-1888), 4th and G; Breese & Company, (1889-1890), 669 4th, downtown.
Lyford L. Dexter, (1887-1888), McGurck Block, downtown San Diego.
A.W. Evans, (1889-1900), 951 6th, downtown San Diego.
Schuebel & Flattery, (1889-1890), 758-760 4th, downtown San Diego.
W.W.Whitson & Co., (1889-1903), 4th and E, and 1219 Plaza, downtown San Diego.
Witherby & Johnson, (1889), 907 6th, downtown San Diego.
Bradley & Woolman, (1905-1920), NW Corner 7th, and 1544 C, downtown San Diego.
Davis & Anderson, O.N. Davis & Co., (1905-1909), 1912 Plaza, downtown San Diego.

J.T. Barkely, 3rd and Ash (1910-1916), 1466 4th (1917-1920), in downtown San Diego.

Hambley & Co., Hambley & Smith, Hambley Smith Murphy, (1910-1918), 1219 Plaza, 4th and Cedar, and 1570 4th, downtown San Diego.

E.H. Stokes, (1911-1920), La Mesa

Barkley & Brower, (1912-1913), El Cajon

Furlong & Company, (1914), 246 Cedar Street, downtown San Diego

H.C. Carmichael & Co., Carmichael & McMahan, McMahan & Davis, Carmichael, Thurston & Co., (1915-1920), 3rd and Ash, downtown San Diego (see more about this company below).

Benbough Funeral Parlors, (1918-1920), 7th and Date; 725 Date, downtown San Diego.

Hemstock & Davis, (1915), Davis - Clatworthy Co. (1916), Davis Undertaking Company, (1917-1920), 1752 4th, downtown and east San Diego, Davis Undertaking Company, (1920), 4182 University.

H.W. Merkley, (1916), 3757 5th, University Undertaking Parlors (H.W. Merkley), (1916-1918), University Undertaking Parlors, (1919-1920), 3655 5th, Hillcrest. This mortuary is still in business.

Smith, Murphy & Randall, (1917-1918), 6th and Cedar & 538 Cedar, Smith, Randall, Meacham Co., (1919-1920), 538 Cedar, downtown San Diego

The San Diego Genealogical Society has for sale a book entitled *Johnson Saum and Nobel Mortuary Records: 1869-February 1888, 1907-1909*. The mortuary records give year, name, date of death, age at death, place of birth, sex, marital status, and disposition ("shipped East", "bur Catholic Cem Old Town", etc.) The records from 1907 to 1908 are more complete, giving date of death, name, age at death, race, nativity, sex, marital status, cause of death, physician, where buried, and place of death.

The San Diego Genealogical Society has also published records from H.C. Carmichael & Co. mortuary in *Leaves and Saplings*. Most burials are for Catholic individuals and include date and location of birth and death, age at death, date of burial, where buried, and parents and spouses, where available.

The Family History has a citation for *Goodbody Funeral Home: Permits for Burial and Removal 1913-1919 and Funeral Home Records from 1914-1921*, Film No. 1598078. This film can be ordered from the Family History Center at Salt Lake City and viewed at the local Family History Center. The Goodbody Funeral Home records were in the possession of Bernard Goodbody and may be an excellent source for Catholic burials in San Diego for this funeral home was in operation for many years and served the Catholic community. The Goodbody records include name, age, sex, residence, name and birthplace of parents, spouse, dates of birth and death, and county burial permits. The source of these records is listed as the "San Diego County Registrar".

Cemetery Records

In discussing the cemeteries of San Diego, I rely on and am very grateful to Laurie Bissell for her article entitled "San Diego Cemeteries: A Brief Guide," *Journal of San Diego History*, Volume XXVIII (Fall 1982), pp. 269-291; Fred Rimbach, Jr., who wrote "A History of the Cemeteries of the City of San Diego, California," (San Diego: Fred Jay Rimbach, Jr., 1949), the manuscript of which is in the California Room of the downtown San Diego Public Library, and other authors mentioned in this section.

Presidio/Mission San Diego Cemeteries

Laurie Bissell writes, p. 270: "On July 1, 1769, soon after the arrival of [Father Junipero] Serra, burials began in consecrated ground on Presidio Hill. ... Even though people began moving off Presidio Hill and settled in Old Town, burials still took place within the Presidio walls. These burials included early settlers as well as Mission Indians. The last recorded burial in this location was Henry Delano Fitch who died in 1849, the same year as the first burial at El Campo Santo in Old Town. ... Although it was no longer used by Europeans, the Indians continued burying their dead on Presidio Hill through the 1870s."[10]

As mentioned above under "Death and Burial Records," burials at the cemetery on Presidio Hill include well known San Diego historical figures. Fred Rimbach states, in the section of his manuscript on Presidio

Hill Cemetery: "Henry D. Fitch, born May 7, 1799, died January 13, 1849, at 4:00 o'clock and 20 minutes in the afternoon, was buried on Presidio Hill (1849). Jose R. Carrillo and Jose Maria Estudillo were buried on Presidio Hill; Carrillo on November 10, 1809 and Estudillo on April 9, 1830. Sylvester Pattie, pathfinder, leader of the first party of Americans into Alta California over Southern trails, arrived at San Diego Presidio, March 27, 1828. Died near the present Serra Museum on Presidio Hill, April 24, 1828. He was the first American buried in California soil."[11]

Others identified in archeological excavations as having been buried on Presidio Hill include Henry Delano Fitch's daughter Natalia, Joseph Francis Snook, the possible burial of Josef Manuel Arroyo (who was killed in the Indian raid on Mission San Diego in 1775) and two children of Felipe Romero. There is an excellent article by the late Dr. Paul Ezell entitled "The Excavation Program at the San Diego Presidio", *Journal of San Diego History*, Volume XXII (Fall 1976) which discusses the excavation of the graves of Fitch and others. This article also contains citations to additional journal articles on this subject. The article can be accessed on the Internet by typing "San Diego Historical Society" into Google or another search engine, clicking on "Journal" and requesting the article by name or author.

Please note that the cemetery on Presidio Hill has been grassed over and is now Presidio Park. There are no tombstones available for viewing there and no indication of where people were buried.

There are also individuals buried at Mission San Diego de Alcala. Burials for the Presidio and Mission are included in R. Clinton Griffin's *Mission San Diego de Alcala: Burials for Mission and Presidio: 1775 - 1831*, as mentioned in "Death and Burial Records" above. Copies of this book are available at San Diego Historical Society and possibly at the El Cajon Family History Center, 1270 So. Orange Avenue, El Cajon, California. Ph: (619) 588-1426. More often than not, Hispanic soldiers, settlers and their families were buried on Presidio Hill, while Indian adults and children were buried at the mission.

As with Presidio Hill, there are no tombstones at Mission San Diego de Alcala and no indication of where people are buried, except that several priests are buried under the altar at the mission, among them Fr. Luis Jaume, who died in the Indian raid on the mission in November, 1775. Fr. Jaume was first buried on Presidio Hill and was later reinterred at the mission.

At the end of the R. Clinton Griffin book for Mission San Diego de Alcala and Presidio Hill is a listing of U.S. soldiers buried at the mission from 1850 to 1858, including the following:

Diego (James) Burns, died 24 April 1854
John Condon, died 31 January 1853
Joseph Denny, died 10 March 1852
William Hayes, died 31 January 1853
Thomas L. Huxford, died 19 September 1852
Frederick Hyer, died 30 May 1858
Henry Johnson, died 22 July 1852
Lawrence Kearney, died 19 June 1850
*Richard Kerren, died 06 November 1856
Michael Malley, died 23 August 1855
Patrick Nagle, died 10 June 1855
James Newlands, died 16 March 1852
Jeremiah O'Sullivan, died 08 September 1852
Thomas Roger, died 03 August 1856
Michael Ross, died 10 August 1852
William Smith, died 01 June 1857
*George Williams, died 05 February 1851

Soldiers with an asterisk before their names were reinterred in the cemetery of the original military reservation now called Fort Rosecrans National Cemetery, located on Point Loma in San Diego.

These soldiers arrived with others who were serving in the Mexican War. For lack of living quarters, they took up residence in the old Mission San Diego de Alcala which, at that time, was falling into ruin. Richard Kerren was a colorful historical figure who left a wife and many children when he died. There is a *Journal of San Diego History* article written about him as well as a thesis at the University of San Diego. To access the *Journal of San Diego History* article on the Internet, type "San Diego Historical Society" into

Google or another search engine, click on "Journal", and request the article on Richard Kerren.

El Campo Santo at Old Town

El Campo Santo Cemetery was created when Presidio Hill families moved down the hill to found Old Town. Laurie Bissell states, p. 271: "San Diego's second oldest cemetery, El Campo Santo, dates back to 1849 with the burial of Juan Adams. Burials continued through 1880, consisting of early San Diegans from varied backgrounds."[12] Members of the Bandini, Osuna, Pedrorena, Estudillo and Aguirre families are buried at this cemetery.

Burials at El Campo Santo were documented by Lawrence Riveroll and Orion M. Zink (see "Books Containing Cemetery Information, discussed below.) The R. Clinton Griffin Collection includes a book entitled *El Campo Santo Cemetery [The Holy Field], San Diego, California: Burials 1849-1880* which is available at the San Diego Historical Society and possibly at the El Cajon Family History Center Library, 1270 So. Orange Avenue, El Cajon, CA. Ph: (619) 588-1426.

Also, upon entering El Campo Santo cemetery, you will see a listing on display of individuals who are buried at there. A number of burials could not be identified, however, including some that were paved over to create San Diego Avenue, which is adjacent to the cemetery. There are several original tombstones at El Campo Santo, but the wooden crosses are of recent vintage.

San Pasqual Cemetery at Old Town

There was a cemetery at Old Town where Americans who died at the Battle of San Pasqual (in the Mexican War) were buried. According to Orion Zink, the location of this cemetery was in Block 540 of Old Town on Pascoe's Map of 1870, a block which was unnumbered in the Cave Couts' survey of 1849. These burials were later reinterred at Fort Rosecrans National Cemetery on Point Loma. Contact this cemetery for a list of the men from the Battle of San Pasqual who are buried there. There may also be a plaque in the older portion of this cemetery which lists the names of these soldiers.

Protestant Cemetery at La Playa

From the founding of San Diego in 1769 until the early 1840s, cemeteries generally contained only burials of Catholic individuals. But when traders from the eastern seaboard and other countries began arriving in San Diego from the early 1820s to 1846, the need for a Protestant Cemetery at La Playa, the historic port of San Diego, was felt. The need grew more acute with the advent of the Mexican War in 1846 and when settlers and Gold Rush enthusiasts began appearing in San Diego in 1849.

The Protestant Cemetery at La Playa was the first of two small Protestant cemeteries to be established to accommodate these individuals. These two cemeteries were used for the burial of Protestants until Mount Hope Cemetery became available for burials in 1869.

The Protestant Cemetery at La Playa was located half way up the bay side of Point Loma near La Playa, and when Lt. Cave Couts surveyed La Playa in 1849, he left Block 43 off the survey map when he found out that a cemetery was in use at that location. Block 43 and all of old La Playa south of Kellogg Street is now within the Point Loma Military Reservation and cannot be accessed for security reasons. The cemetery was never moved, but some of the bodies may have been reinterred elsewhere. A narrow road, built on an unknown date, bisected this cemetery, and its actual location is known only to one or two archeologists who have conducted studies on the military reservation.

The use of this cemetery for the burial of those who died aboard ships was mentioned in William Smythe's *History of San Diego*, where he states, on p. 242: "J.M. Julian, in later days editor of the *San Diegan*, was in San Diego Bay on May 4, 1850, on board the steamer *Panama*, en route to the Isthmus. The steamer stopped to bury a passenger who died en route and to examine the bay in the interest of the steamship company."[13]

Three people were known to have been buried in Protestant Cemetery at La Playa in 1847, and all three arrived with the Mormon Battalion which came to San Diego to relieve U.S. Troops during the Mexican War. Eugene Russell, a volunteer with the Mormon Battalion, may have been the first of the Mormon contingent to be buried at Protestant Cemetery in La Playa. Russell died of typhoid on March 10, 1847.

In a book entitled *A Doctor Comes to California: The Diary of John S. Griffin*, available at the San Diego Historical Society, Dr. Griffin is quoted on p. 74 as having written: "27th Febry. I still remain at San Diego--in charge of the Hospital--having only two sick dragoons Streeter and Child. ... A man by name [Eugene] Russell--A Volunteer has been in hospital for two weeks--with Typhoid Fever--he had been sick for some time previous to being admitted." On p. 76 is stated: "10th March--The man Russell died of the fever...."[14] Dr. Griffin did not indicate where Russell was buried, but as two others below who came with the Mormon Battalion were buried at Protestant Cemetery at La Playa, it is possible that Russell was buried there also.

The second person to be buried at Protestant Cemetery from the Mormon Battalion was Lydia Edmonds Hunter, the wife of Capt. Jesse Hunter of Co. B, Mormon Battalion, who was born 22 January 1823 and died 27 April 1847, either of the flu, "Quotidian Fever" or typhoid, depending on which diarist of the times is consulted. About two weeks before her death, Mrs. Hunter had given birth to a son named Diego Hunter, the first child of American parents to be born in San Diego. The second individual was Albert Warren Dunham, a private in Co. B, Mormon Battalion, who was born on 23 May 1828 and died 10 May 1847. Dunham succumbed to inflammation of the brain or a brain ulcer.

Their burials at Protestant Cemetery in La Playa were confirmed by "The Diary of Robert S. Bliss, Company "B" Mormon Battalion, U.S. Army, 1846-1847," available at San Diego Historical Society. On p. 18 is stated: "Tues 27th Last night our Capt was bereaved of his Wife who left a Babe to his care born last Tues 1 week ago; She was buried in the foreign buring Ground near the Shiping or Harbour." On p. 19 is stated: "Tues 11 Last night one of our company Died of Inflammation on the brain (Albert Dunham) he was buried in the American burying ground at the Harbour."[15]

Death notices began appearing in the *San Diego Herald*, San Diego's first newspaper, and the San Diego Genealogical Society transcribed notices from this newspaper from June 5, 1851 through March 5, 1859 into a publication entitled *Newspaper Records: Vital Statistics From San Diego Newspapers: 1851-1885* (SDNR). Among these notices were some likely candidates for burial at La Playa's Protestant Cemetery, although these individuals could have been buried elsewhere. [Note: underlined dates in the listings below are the dates the notice appeared in the newspaper]:

5 June 1851, At the Playa, S.D., 1 June 1851, William Valesch of Baltimore. (SDNR, p. 5-A)

2 Oct 1851, At the Playa, 30 Sept 1851, Henry Lindsey, aged 38. (SDNR, p. 5-A)

16 Oct 1851, On board *S.S. California* at sea. 27 Sept 1851, John De Camp son of Jas. C. and Ellen De Camp late of St. Louis, Mo. Age 9 yrs. 30 days. (SDNR, p. 5-A)

A child of Rev. Thomas H. Pearne, Missionary of the Methodist Church for Oregon. 10 mo. (n.d.) (SDNR, p. 5-A)

Mrs. Mary Flanagan, enroute to join her husband in San Francisco, (n.d.). (SDNR, p. 5-A)

5 Dec 1851 Aboard the *S.S. California*, Samuel D. Corwin, of N.Y. Age 23. 29 Nov. 1851. (SDNR, p. 5-A)

Amos Sawtell of Boston, Mass. Age abt. 48. 29 Nov 1851. (SDNR, p. 5-A)

> 28 Jan 1854, On Ship *Golden Gate* in S.D. bay, (n.d.) Isaac M. Gibson, age abt. 40 yrs. Born Philadelphia. Resided New Orleans abt. 11 yrs before coming to Calif. in 1849. (SDNR, p. 6-A)
>
> 1 Apr 1854, 27 Mar 1854 on board U.S. Sloop of War *Portsmouth* in harbor of San Diego, Nicholas Turner (colored) of Wash. D.C. (SDNR, p. 6-A)

A good source of information about who was buried at La Playa's Protestant Cemetery is the diary of Rev. Matthew Simpson, excerpts of which were published in an article entitled "Matthew Simpson's Diary: A Wednesday in San Diego, 1854," *Journal of San Diego History*, Vol. 29, No. 3 (Summer 1983), which can be accessed by typing "San Diego Historical Society" into Google or another search engine, clicking on "Journals" and requesting the article by the name Matthew Simpson or the title of the article. The article, on pp. 222-223, states:

> "The buildings at the harbor are few in number but generally frame and are occupied by Americans or foreigners. A few drinking houses--a warehouse or two--and two or three residences compose this part of town. Here stand the hide houses spoken of in Dana's *Two Years Before the Mast*.
>
> "But with me the greatest object of interest was a little cemetery on the hill side--for there is a high hill with reddish soil rising back of the landing, and forming the high ground of the peninsula. Nearly half way up this slope are about 40 graves of those who have died at sea, and have been buried in the last few years. About 1/2 have no boards to tell whose they are--Others have simple head boards with the name or name & age, and state from whence inscribed--and three or four in addition are surrounded by little poled inclosures.
>
> "A few of the names I noted on my memorandum, R. Bradley, on board the *Congress* '47--R. Adams '47--the next was that of a lady--the only one marked--I copied it 'In memory of Mary Jane Sandey, wife of Wm. A. Sandey, who was born in the town of Cherryfield, Mass. Anno. 1828 and who departed this life on board the ship Monterey in the harbor of San Diego on the 25th of August 1850 age 22 years--'Behold my friends as you pass bye, As you are now so once was I. As I am now so you must be. Prepare for death and follow me.'
>
> "As I stared at her grave, thoughts of her home, her father & mother--the bridal home--golden dreams--sad hours of sickness and the loneliness of death, passed in review before me.
>
> "There too was the grave of a child of 5 yrs over which was inscribed a simple cross. In one enclosure slept Sautill of Boston and Caniz of N. York--who died in California in 1851, the first as I learned from one who was with him when he died leaving at home a wife & 6 children--possessed once of property he had been unfortunate, and was seeking to repair his fortunes by an adventure in California--but by Panama fever he & his associates in death were smitten down, while 150 others were sick of same fever.
>
> "Next was the grave of J. A. Sawyer, Master of the vessel *Newton* of New Bedford who died in '44 age 34--Then Neil McClullen of ship *Congress* who was killed by a fall from the Royal Mast Head aged 18. There was a row of graves which interested me because of the singular mingling from places so remote--J. Cart from Indiana Feby. 11, 52 aged 28. Tyler--Michigan--Miller--Rhode Island--Howes Maine '52 (Miss or Mass) I think the latter, but memorandum book looks like former) Allen, Vermont--I thought how strangely were these young men united in death."[16]

The following notice of death appeared in the *San Diego Herald* for December 5, 1851: "Amos Sawtell of Boston, Mass. Age abt. 48. 29 Nov. 1851." This notice confirms at least one of Rev. Simpson's diary entries. Visitors to California in the late 1840s and early 1850s or those who died "at the Playa" in the early years may also have been buried in La Playa's Protestant Cemetery.

There were two gravesites uncovered at Protestant Cemetery in La Playa in 1949, according to notes of historian Ben Dixon. The tentative conclusions were that the skeletons were males, one of about 35 years of age, who were 5'5" and 5'7" tall approximately. There was no evidence of violent death in either case.

Protestant Cemetery at Old Town
Old Town San Diego was first settled by descendants of the early Hispanic founders of California. These individuals first lived on Presidio Hill adjacent to Old Town, but after Mexican independence from Spain in 1821 they moved down the hill to found Old Town. Hispanic Catholics buried their dead first at the old cemetery on Presidio Hill, at Mission San Diego de Alcala in Mission Valley, and after 1849 at El Campo Santo in Old Town.

A small Protestant Cemetery was begun at Old Town in 1850, and it is listed on the San Diego Historical Site Board Register of Historical Sites. According to Orion Zink, who was shown the location by two pioneers, this cemetery was in Block 515 of the Pascoe map of 1870 or Block 92 of the Lt. Cave Couts survey of Old Town in 1849. The cemetery was bounded by Ampudia Street on the north, Moore Street on the east, Trias Street on the south, and the old waterline of the San Diego River on the west. It is now covered over by Interstate 5 freeway at the approximate location of the "Old Town" exit. Orion Zink also noted that the San Pasqual Cemetery was in Block 540, the block just south of Protestant Cemetery, an unnumbered block on the Cave Couts survey of 1849.

Laurie Bissell states about Old Town's Protestant Cemetery, pp. 271-272: "Alcalde Joshua H. Bean deeded land to Adolphis Savin on February 18, 1850 (see Deed Book A, p. 67 covering all four lots of Block 92 of the Couts survey of 1849). Savin sold it to Juan Bandini and William Heath Davis a month later (see Deed Book B, pp. 35, 36, 37 and 40, covering Lots 4, 3, 1 and 2, respectively, of the Couts Survey of 1849). Soon after San Diego Protestants began to bury their dead there. As San Diego's population moved away from Old Town, relatives of those buried on this land in 'Protestant Cemetery' began to transfer their dead to other cemeteries."[17]

Laurie Bissell continues that there were at least four known burials at Protestant Cemetery in Old Town: Tommie Whaley, infant son of Thomas Whaley of Old Town, Francis "Jack" Hinton, Frank Ames, and Francis Steele, and these individuals will be discussed below.

The best evidence of burials at Protestant Cemetery in Old Town is found in the San Diego Genealogical Society's publication *Johnson Saum & Nobel Mortuary Records: 1869-February 1888, 1907-1909*, hereafter ("MR"). This book includes many burials for Mount Hope Cemetery, El Campo Santo and Calvary cemeteries, the old Jewish Cemetery at Point Loma, and the Masonic and Odd Fellows Cemeteries which later were absorbed into Mount Hope Cemetery. The publication also lists several burials at Protestant Cemetery in Old Town.

The Johnson Saum & Nobel records are augmented by records presented in two additional San Diego Genealogical Society publications: death notices in *Newspaper Records: Vital Statistics from San Diego Newspapers, 1851-1885* (hereafter "SDNR") and burial notices in *Episcopal Church Records: Holy Trinity Episcopal and St. Pauls Episcopal*, particularly burials from Holy Trinity Church, the first Episcopal church in San Diego (hereafter "HT").

The records below reflect burials at Protestant Cemetery in Old Town. Please note that the underlined date is the date the notice appeared in the newspaper. "MR" records are from the Johnson Saum & Nobel mortuary book; "SDNR" records are from the San Diego Newspaper Records book; and "HT" records are from the Holy Trinity Episcopal Church book. All records for an individual from the above sources are combined below into the following:

U S Soldier, d. 11 Feb (1870) San Diego, 35 yrs, b. not known, sgl, bu. Protestant Cem Old Town. (MR, p. 2)

Capt Geo A Pendleton, d. 5 Mar (1871) San Diego, 50 yrs, b. ..., bu. Protestant Cem Old Town. (MR, p. 4) Newspaper death notice reads: <u>9 Mar 1871</u> Died. In Old S.D. 3 Mar. Capt. George Allan Pendleton, Co. Clerk of S.D. b. 1823 in Bowling Green, Caroline Co., Va., Landed in Cal. 5 May 1847. Biography. (SDNR, p. 16) [Note: George Pendleton was a prominent figure at Old Town and his first wife was an Estudillo. He owned the Derby-Pendleton House which is still standing at Old Town and he was the County Clerk and Recorder for a number of years.

James W. Cullen, d 18 Nov (1873), 35 yrs, b. NY, mar, bu Protestant Cem Old Town. (MR, p. 10) Newspaper notice reads: <u>14 Dec 1873</u> Died. In Old San Diego, Dec. 12, James W. Cullen. (SDNR, p. 31)

Mrs Dodson, d 9 Dec (1874), b____, bu Protestant Cem Old Town. (MR, p. 12) Newspaper death notice reads: <u>10 Dec 1874</u> Died. At Old San Diego, December 8, Matilda, wife of N.H. Dodson. (SDNR, p. 38)

William Evans, d 8 Jan (1876), 56 yrs, b England, sgl, bu Protestant Cem Old Town. (MR, p. 15)

Child of A L Seeley, d 15 Mar (1876), 1 mo, b San Diego, male, bu Protestant Cem Old Town. (MR, p.15) Holy Trinity Church burial record reads: Cecilia Seeley, 16 Mar 1876, Protestant Cem., Old Town, 1 mo. (HT, p. 16-B) [Note: Albert Seeley, Cecilia Seeley's father, renovated the famous Bandini House at Old Town, added a second floor, and opened the Cosmopolitan House hotel, stables and a stage line there. Notes in Old Town State Park files indicate that Seeley, from Marshall, Clark County, Illinois, married Emily Walker, born in 1835 in Manchester, England. They had six children, one adopted.]

Henrietta Huick, d 19 Apr, 52 yrs, b Germany, wid, bu Protestant Cem Old Town. (MR, p. 16) Holy Trinity Church burial record reads: Henrietta Heuck, 20 Apr 1876, Protestant Cem., Old Town, 45 yrs. (HT, p. 16-B) Newspaper death notice reads: <u>20 Apr 1876</u> Died. Heuce. At Old Town Apr 12 of pulmonary consumption Mrs. Henrietta Heuce, age about 45 years. Funeral this (Thursday) afternoon at 2 o'clock from her late residence. (SDNR, p. 49)

Two burials "at Old Town" were recorded in the Johnson Saum and Nobel records and/or Holy Trinity Church records and these two burials may also have taken place at Old Town's Protestant Cemetery:

Florence Seeley, bu 19 Mar 2 years, b San Diego, bu near house, Old Town. (MR, p. 40). Holy Trinity Church record reads: Florence Seeley, ____ 1885, Old Town, infant. (HT, p. 17-B) [Note: Johnson Saum and Nobel records previously indicated that a sister of Florence Seeley was buried at Protestant Cemetery in Old Town. Perhaps Florence Seeley was also buried there].

John Lee's Holy Trinity Church record reads: 15 Mar 1886, Old Town, 42 yrs. (HT, p. 18-B)

Laurie Bissell discusses four others who were buried at Protestant Cemetery in Old Town, and two of these burials were included in newspaper and other records as follows:

<u>30 Jan 1858</u>, In S.D. 29 Jan 1858, Thomas, second son of Thomas and Anna E. Whaley. Age 1 yr. 5 mo. 11 da. (SDNR, p. 7-A) [Note: Thomas Whaley, Sr. was born in New York City in 1823, arrived in California during the Gold Rush, and in 1853, returned to New York to marry Anna E. Lannay. He was a prominent merchant at Old Town who built a large brick house there for his family which is still standing.]

30 June 1870 Died. At his res. near San Luis Rey, 26 June, Francis Hinton, ae 52. b 9 Sep 1818, Rondaut, Duchess Co., N.Y. Arrived in Cal. 1848. Business, Hinton & Hooper at Ft. Yuma. Biography. (SDNR, p. 13)

[Note: Abraham Ten Eyck De Witt Hornbeck left New York State, changed his name to Francis Hinton, and became a merchant after his arrival at San Diego. He later moved to Yuma, Arizona, to operate a store there in conjunction with George Hooper, and in the last years of his life he owned Rancho Agua Hedionda in north San Diego County, having obtained it from the Marron family. He willed the property to Robert Kelly, his overseer, and when Kelly died the property was divided up among his relatives.]

Laurie Bissell also indicates that Frank Ames and Francis Steele were buried at Protestant Cemetery in Old Town, and while no notices of their deaths were found, both left considerable estates and their graves were suitably marked with headstones.

On the Ames tombstone appeared this inscription: "Sacred to the memory of Frank Ames, son of Samuel and Anne Ames. Born in Providence, R.I. March 14, 1811 and died in San Diego June 20, 1861. Aged 50 yrs, 3 months and 6 days. If honest worth a place in Heaven may find, Poor Frank left not without his passport signed. [On the other was this wording]: Sacred to the memory of Francis Steele, who died Jan. 17 1860, aged 32 years."[18] These two individuals were reinterred at Mount Hope Cemetery in 1937 and the tombstone of Frank Ames was also stored at Mount Hope.

It is unknown where the following individuals from the *San Diego Herald* death notices were buried, but they may have been buried at Protestant Cemetery in Old Town rather than Protestant Cemetery in La Playa because Old Town was the more established location at the time, and more people lived there during the 1850s. Of course, as mentioned above for Protestant Cemetery in La Playa, these individuals may have been buried elsewhere. Note: the underlined date is the date the notice appeared in the newspaper:

28 Aug 1851, At New S.D., 27 Aug 1851, Thomas L. Pickering formerly of Portsmouth, N.H. Age 36 yrs. (SDNR, p. 5-A). [Note: Thomas Pickering was a carpenter who helped to erect the first wooden houses at New San Diego, a harbor location established in 1850 in what is now downtown San Diego, a few miles south of Old Town.]

3 Dec 1853, In S.D., 29 Nov 1853, Frederick J. Painter, M.D., formerly of N.Y. Age 35 yrs. (SDNR, p. 6-A) [Note: Dr. Painter was one of the first doctors at Old Town San Diego.]

28 Jan 1854, In S.D. 24 Jan 1854, William Green of Chester Co., Pa. Age abt. 54 yrs. (SDNR, p. 6-A)

28 Apr 1855, 25 Apr 1855, Gustave Fischer in S.D. Age 49. (SDNR, p. 6-A)

17 Nov 1855, In this city, 17 Nov 1855, Sarah R. wife of H.C. Ladd. Age 30. (SDNR, p. 6-A)

29 Mar 1856, In S.D. 24 Mar 1856, Sophia Fischer, widow of the late Gustave Fischer. Age 32 yrs. (SDNR, p. 6-A)

29 Nov 1856, In S.D. 23 Nov 1856, Lydia A. Morse, wife of E.W. Morse, Esq. Age 28 yrs. (SDNR, p. 7-A) [Note: Lydia Gray was the first wife of Ephraim Weed Morse. Both were from Amesbury, Massachusetts, where Morse was born in 1823, and they were married in 1851. Morse was an important San Diego merchant, public official and attorney, who arrived in California aboard the *Leonora* in 1849. He came to San Diego in early 1850.]

14 Mar 1857, At San Luis Rey, 7 Mar 1857, John Curry of New Hampshire. Age abt. 25 yrs. Buried in S.D. (SDNR, p. 7-A)

24 Oct 1857, In S.D. 18 Oct 1857, Frederick Emell. Age 46. (SDNR, p. 7-A)

19 Dec 1857, In S.D. 12 Dec 1857, Henry youngest son of James Donahoe. Age 2 yrs. 2 mo. 14 days. (SDNR, p. 7-A) [Note: In the early to mid-1850s, James Donohoe was an storekeeper at La Playa and Old Town. It was said that he became wealthy and moved with his family to San Francisco.]

19 Dec.1857, 14 Dec 1857, Phoebe, dau. of H.C. Ladd. Age 12 yrs. 2 mo. 17 da. In S.D. (SDNR, p. 7-A)

9 Jan 1858, In S.D. 6 Jan 1858, John Haight. Age abt. 40 yrs. (SDNR, p. 7-A)

17 July 1858, In S.D. 13 July 1858, George P., youngest son of George B. Tolman. Age 1 yr. 8 mo. 20 days. (SDNR, p. 7-A)

5 Feb 1859, 3 Feb 1859, Judge William H. Moon, native of Richmond Co., Ga. Age 58 yrs. (SDNR, p. 7-A)

5 Mar 1859, In S.D. 3 Mar 1859, James Daniels. Age 33 yrs. Native of N.Y. (SDNR, p. 7-A)

The following death notices in *The San Diego Union* contained likely candidates for burial at Protestant Cemetery in Old Town. Death notices from this newspaper were only transcribed up to 1870 below because by then Mount Hope Cemetery became the predominant burial location for Protestants. Note: the underlined date is the date the death notice appeared in the newspaper]

24 Oct 1868 Died. At San Diego, on the 21st Oct., Isaac Collins, aged 38 or 40 years. (SDNR,p.8)

23 Jan 1869 Died. At S.D., 18 Jan 1869, G.W. Marchant, ae 40 yrs. Rochester, N.Y. and Oregon papers, please copy. (SDNR, p. 9)

20 Feb 1869 Died. 14 Feb Joseph, infant son of Robert & Mary A. Israel, ae 4 yrs. (SDNR, p. 9)

6 Mar 1869 Died. At New Town, 5 Mar 1869, S. Shearer, son of Judge Shearer, of Oakland, ae abt 30 yrs. (SDNR, p. 9)

7 July 1869 Died. In S.D. 30 June 1869, Joseph Warren Russel, ae 36 yrs. b. in Salem, Mass. Salem papers please copy. (SDNR, p. 10)

18 Aug 1869 Died. At the Bay View House, New S.D., 16 Aug, John Givelin, age 41 yrs. English and Welsh papers please copy. (SDNR, p. 10)

22 Sep 1869 Died. In New S.D. on the 18th inst., Willie Finlie, infant son of W.F. and Augusta W. Pettit. (SDNR, p. 11)

6 Oct 1869 Died. In New S.D., 27 Sep, Mrs. Lizzie M. Shaw, wife of F.M. Shaw. (SDNR, p. 11)

13 Oct 1869 Died. In New S.D. 6 Oct 1869, Mrs. Julia Frances Dyer, wife of H.C. Dyer. Age 29 yrs 6 mo. San Francisco and N.Y. papers please copy. Mr. Dyer, messenger of Wells, Fargo & Co's. Express Co. Mrs. came to San Diego "a few weeks since." (SDNR, p. 11)

<u>24 Mar 1870</u> Died. In S.D. 17 Mar, Mary Ellen, dau of Mr. W.H. Weddle, ae 5. (SDNR, p. 12)

<u>31 Mar 1870</u> Died. In S.D. 30 Mar, George Eisen, late of San Francisco. (SDNR, p. 12)

<u>18 Aug 1870</u> Died. In S.D., 30 July, James Henry Little, ae 39 yrs, 4 mo. Rockford, Ill. papers please copy. (SDNR, p. 13)

<u>1 Sep 1870</u> Died. In S.D., 29 Aug, infant dau of John M. & Addie S. Boyd. (SDNR, p. 13)

<u>15 Dec 1870</u> Died. In S.D. 8 Dec, Eva Bell, dau of G.W. & Nancy Cofer, ae 18 mo 2 weeks. Sonoma Co. papers please copy. (SDNR, p. 15)

There were several burials at Mount Hope Cemetery which were "brought from Old Town" on March 10, 1890. The burial location where these burials were reinterred was owned by James McCoy, a prominent Old Town historical figure who died in the 1850s. The individuals reinterred, possibly from Protestant Cemetery at Old Town, were included in the San Diego Genealogical Society's publication *Mt. Hope Cemetery Burial Records 1869-1909* (MH), and they were:

Thomas Fox, d. 1890, bur. Mar 10, 1890, white, 50y, male, b. Ireland, bur. in Div 1 Sec 2 Lot 14, Remains brought from Old Town. (MH, p. 239)

Francis Hinton (Remains of) d. Jun 26, 1870, bur. Mar 10, 1890, white, 53, male, b. American, bur. in Div 1 Sec 2 Lot 14, Remains brought from Old Town. [See his first burial record above.] (MH, p. 267)

J.A. Lee (Remains of), d. abt. 1886, bur. Mar 10, 1890, white, 33, male, b. American, bur. in Div 1 Sec 2 Lot 14, Remains brought from Old Town. [Note: See his first burial record above.] (MH, p. 311)

Anne Jane Rourke (Remains of) d. 22 Sep 1887, bur. Mar 10, 1890, white, 68 yrs, female, married, b. Ireland, bur. in Div 1 Sec 2 Lot 14, Remains brought from Old Town. (MH, p. 383)

Two other burials are at the same location at Mount Hope, a J. Rourke and an E. Baxter, but no mention is made of these individuals in San Diego Genealogical Society's transcription of Mount Hope records.

Augustus S. Ensworth, an attorney who resided at Old Town in the 1850s and the early 1860s, was taking care of Thomas Whaley's property while Whaley lived at San Francisco. Ensworth frequently wrote to Whaley and updated him on what was happening at Old Town, and some of his letters appear in the files of Old Town San Diego State Historic Park. In a May 21, 1862 letter to Whaley, Ensworth states:

"Please send me the inclosed bill of lumber. Since making it out, a thought struck me: the grave of your little boy is within two or three feet of Mr. Ames grave. If you choose to have it fenced in, then send me down about as much against lumber. Mr. Ames' estate pays one third to you and myself."[19]

But it was in an earlier letter to Thomas Whaley, dated September 12, 1861, that Ensworth revealed his desire to be buried at Protestant Cemetery in Old Town. In that letter, Ensworth writes:

"...I am now growing old quite fast, and am contented to remain here and be buried in this graveyard by the side of Ames. This reminds me of stones for his grave, which you will send. Place on the headstone the following: Sacred to the memory of Frank Ames, son of Sam L. and Anne Ames, born in Providence, R.I. March 14, 1811 and died in San Diego June 20th 1861,

Aged--Years--Months--Days. Of course, the above is not arranged as it should be on the stone. Arrange it to suit yourself."[20]

Unfortunately, as things turned out, Squire Ensworth was buried at Old Calvary Cemetery in Los Angeles after being cared for in his final days at a hospital run at the Pueblo of Los Angeles by Catholic nuns. The gravestone of Frank Ames is no longer stored at Mount Hope Cemetery. And the two old Protestant Cemeteries of San Diego have now disappeared from view, taking with them countless memories of times gone by.

Old Jewish Cemetery
Laurie Bissell writes, p. 272: "The first [person of Jewish descent] in San Diego, Louis Rose, arrived in 1850. Immediately he began to purchase land, eventually developing 'Roseville.' Soon more Jews settled in San Diego. By 1861, they organized Adath Joshurun under the leadership of Marcus Schiller. Top priority would be acquiring land for a Jewish cemetery. Louis Rose answered the need by deeding Adath Joshurun five acres in Roseville. Marcus Schiller and Joseph Mannasse provided the lumber to fence the land, and the community planted about fifty pepper trees. Both Rose and Mannasse were among those buried in the cemetery."[21] Laurie Bissell adds that some burials were reinterred at Home of Peace Cemetery, which was started in 1892.

According to Orion Zink's notes, the old Jewish cemetery was located around the 2900 block of Fordham Street near where Sharp Hospital is now located in the Midway district of San Diego. Orion Zink continues: "Among those buried there were Jacob Mannasse and Louis Rose. Mannasse was buried there Feb. 2, 1854 [1864?] and Louis Rose, Feb. 14, 1888. The funeral services for both of these men were conducted by San Diego Masonic Lodge No. 35... [Note: could Zink mean 1864 for the first burial? His date is seven years before the Adath Joshurun congregation was started in 1861]...

"At the time of the housing development in the 1940's, the unidentified bones in this cemetery were reburied in a common grave of the County Section at Mt. Hope Cemetery. In an effort to locate these graves, I contacted Mr. Raymond W. Dehne, the manager of Mt. Hope Cemetery. His records failed to show the reburial of the bones...of Mannasse and Rose."[22] There is a tombstone now marking a gravesite for Louis Rose at Home of Peace Cemetery, which is adjacent to Mount Hope Cemetery. See more information about Home of Peace Cemetery below, which continues this story.

The Johnson Saum Nobel mortuary records include several early burials of Jewish individuals and state that some were buried at "Jewish cem. Old Town." However, since the Adath Joshurun congregation was started around 1861, the burials listed below probably occurred at the Old Jewish Cemetery:

Mrs. Barnett d. 17 Jun (1871) San Diego, 38 yrs, b. ___, mar, bur Jewish cem Old Town. (MR, p. 4).

Klauber, A, Infant of d 22 Aug (1875), 8 mo, b San Diego, female, bu Jewish cem Old Town. (MR, p. 14). Note: later reinterred at Home of Peace Cemetery, Division 13, Lots 23 or 24, Nov. 1893.]

Le Batt, Proff Segemund d 24 Sep. (1881), 57 yrs, b Switzerland, mar, bu Jewish cem. (MR, p. 28).

Carr, Mrs. Celia L. d 9 Apr (1882), 29 years, b Germany, widow, bu Jewish cem. (MR, p 31).

Newburger, Ike d 25 Jul (1883), 35 years, b Germany, sgl, bu Jewish cem. (MR, p. 35).

Shaffer, Bernard d 11 Jul (1884), 32 years, b Russia, sgl, bu Jewish cem. (MR, p. 38).

Klauber, A.L. d 26 Sep (1884), 4 1/2 years, b San Diego, bu Jewish cem, (later removed to Home of Peace Cemetery, Division 13, Lots 23 or 24, in November 1893). (MR, p. 39).

Ables, S.E. d 5 Dec (1885), 45 years, b Germany, sgl, bu Jewish cem. (MR, p. 43).

Green, Henry d 25 Dec (1885), 38 years, b OH, ___, bu Jewish cem. (MR, p. 43).

Cline, infant d 10 Apr (1886), 1 day, b San Diego, bu Jewish cem. (MR, p. 45).

Calvary/Mission Hills Cemetery
Laurie Bissell writes, p. 276: "In 1870, the City of San Diego set aside ten acres of land, bought from Joseph Mannasse, for a cemetery. Half of the cemetery would be for Protestant burials, the other half for the Catholics. The Protestants never used their plot. The Catholic section, said to have been laid out by Father Antonio Ubach, became known as 'Calvary Cemetery.' Many early San Diegans such as the Bandinis and Couts, the Ames and Father Ubach were amongst the 1,650 buried at Calvary."[23]

The count of those who are buried at Calvary Cemetery varies. Many buried there have Hispanic, Irish, and Italian surnames. A factor in the abandonment of Calvary as a burying ground for Protestants was the establishment of Mount Hope Cemetery in 1869. Laurie Bissell adds, p. 276: "With the opening of 'Holy Cross,' a new Catholic cemetery in 1919, Calvary fell to disuse. Burials continued through 1960, but were rare.

"The Catholic Parish of the Immaculate Conception continued to maintain Calvary through 1939, when the City took on the responsibility to provide employment under the W.P.A. Just before the City took over, a fire in the caretaker's shack, located on Calvary grounds, destroyed all the burial records except one book which dated back to 1899. Unmarked graves lost their identity."[24]

Calvary Cemetery has an interesting history. If you go there today, you will see a park. The cemetery was converted into a passive recreation park in 1970. Persons having valid claims to headstones were allowed to remove them and this was done in some cases. However so many buried there were the last of their line or their relatives had moved elsewhere that a majority of the bodies that were buried there are still there. The graves were sodded over after a record was made of the exact locations of the bodies.

Tombstones of historic interest remain at Calvary for they were relocated to an area at the southeast corner of the cemetery adjacent to Grant Elementary School. There is also a memorial plaque nearby which lists those who were identified as having been buried at this cemetery. The memorial plaque and tombstones located in this cemetery can be easily viewed because the cemetery is not fenced.

Photos of many of the tombstones that were at Calvary Cemetery can be found at the Photo Archives of the San Diego Historical Society. The photos are grouped into jackets, and notations on the jackets indicate the section of the cemetery in which the photographs were taken. A researcher can thus locate individual graves within the cemetery from the photo jacket notations.

The best source of information for early burials at Calvary Cemetery is the R. Clinton Griffin burial records included in a volume entitled *Mission San Diego de Alcala: Hills Catholic Cemetery (Old Calvary): 1875-1969*. Look in the index for children's burials, for often the children's listings will add the names of their parents. Copies of this book are available at the San Diego Historical Society Archives and possibly at the El Cajon Family History Center Library, 1270 So. Orange Avenue, El Cajon, CA. Ph: (619) 588-1426.

The following information was mentioned above but bears repeating here. There is a set of burial records compiled by Peter O'Malley, who was a caretaker for Calvary Cemetery. Copies of these records are now at the San Diego Historical Society and the San Diego Genealogical Society and they span a date range of 1897 to 1932. They are in four books:

> A book of cemetery records with the word "Record" on the front cover which includes burials from the late 1900s to around 1930.
>
> A book of cemetery records with the words "ROYAL Memorandum Book Trademark, Pat. Jan. 21, 1890" on the front cover which includes burials from 1913 to 1917.
>
> A book of cemetery records with the word "Composition" on the front cover which includes burials by various funeral homes from 1918 to 1919, with a few burials in the early 1920s.
>
> A book of cemetery records with the word "Exercises" on the front cover which includes burials from approximately 1918 to December, 1932.

The San Diego Historical Society has a copy of a map of Calvary Cemetery which was drawn when the cemetery was being grassed over. It contains many of the burials that took place at Calvary Cemetery, but no one really knows for certain how many individuals were buried there.

Another map for Calvary Cemetery may be in the storage room at Mount Hope Cemetery, and the graves on this map have the names of those buried in individual plots. There is also a drawer of index cards at Mount Hope which contains records of some of those buried at Calvary Cemetery. However, the R. Clinton Griffin collection and the Peter O'Malley records contain a more complete listing of those who are buried at Calvary Cemetery than either the memorial plaque or the index cards at Mount Hope Cemetery.

Mount Hope Cemetery

Mount Hope Cemetery is San Diego's only public cemetery that is currently open. It was established in 1869 by Alonzo E. Horton, the founder of modern downtown San Diego, and others. Mount Hope was named by Augusta Sherman, the wife of Matthew Sherman, a veteran who served in San Diego during the Civil War. Early burials at Mount Hope most often occurred in the G.A.R. Section (for Civil War veterans), in Divisions 1 through 6, and in the Odd Fellows (IOOF) and Masonic sections of the cemetery.

Tombstones in Mount Hope Cemetery date from the 1870s, and contain much information of genealogical interest. There are also several record sources available at the Mount Hope Cemetery office:

> **1. Old cemetery books:** There are four old bound volumes at Mount Hope which constitute a record of early burials to 1948. Burials are grouped by the first letter of the surname and individual burials are listed chronologically under each letter. Volume 1 covers the period of 1869-1909. This volume has been transcribed (though not indexed) by the San Diego Genealogical Society. Volume 2 dates from around 1910-1926; Volume 3 dates from around 1927-1940 and Volume 4 dates from around 1941-1948.
>
> The information in these books varies. The first two books contain more genealogical information, including a decedent's name, date of death, date of burial, race, age at death, sex, marital status, nativity, and location of burial within the cemetery. Some of the nativity listings contain the word "American" but many citations mention the state of birth. The last two books contain only basic burial information, i.e., date of death, date of burial, and location of burial within the cemetery.
>
> **2. Burial cards:** There are about 30 drawers of index cards at Mount Hope Cemetery which provide information on burials. The cards reflect the information in the bound volumes, but have been basically replaced now by a computerized burial information system. "Nativity" was not copied from the bound volumes, so a researcher would have to look at bound volumes to

determine if nativity was listed for their particular ancestor. See also the San Diego Genealogical Society's book *Mount Hope Cemetery Burial Records, Volume 1: 1869-1909* which contains the entire record from the old cemetery burial books (including nativity).

3. Lot or "Legal" cards: These cards show who is buried in a particular lot and also the owner of the lot. The grouping by lot helps a researcher to identify additional family members of an ancestor without having to consult the burial cards or the old cemetery books or maps. The lot cards also contain information about when the lot was first purchased, by whom, and when the people were buried in the lot.

4. Maps: Maps at Mount Hope are valuable because some of the maps list names on individual plots and thus you can see who was buried next to who. Some Mount Hope maps, particularly those for G.A.R. Divisions 1, 2, and 3, show existing tombstones, a valuable clue about whether there is a tombstone which may yield information that can be transcribed. However for the most part there are no tombstones drawn on maps for the other older sections of Mount Hope.

If you believe that a relative may be buried at Mount Hope Cemetery, contact their office at (619) 527-3400 for additional information. Their address is 3751 Market Street, San Diego, CA. 92102. The office is open from 8 a.m. until around 3:30 p.m. M-F and not open on weekends. The grounds are fenced and open every day, but only from 8 a.m to 4 p.m. (not until dusk, like some other San Diego cemeteries). The gates at Mount Hope close at 4:00 p.m. daily.

Cypress View Mausoleum
At the southeast corner of Mount Hope Cemetery is a large structure called Cypress View Mausoleum. It faces away from Mount Hope Cemetery toward Imperial Avenue and is not enclosed by the Mount Hope Cemetery fence. The office is located across the street on Imperial Avenue, and that location also has additional mausoleum crypts.

Brae Canlen, in a April 7, 1988 article in the *San Diego Reader* entitled "Tombstone Territory: The Business of Burial at Mount Hope Cemetery" writes: "State law [did] not allow above-ground graves in public cemeteries, but this was not always the case. In 1927, after years of discussion and debate, the city contracted with a private company to build a mausoleum at Mount Hope. The city was to receive royalties from its operation and retain ultimate authority. Later it was sold to the funeral firm that built it."[25]

Cypress View Mausoleum is currently owned by Bonham Brothers Mortuary. It is one of the nation's largest mausoleums, composed of sanctuaries with burial crypts built above the ground. In the office, there is a file of index cards with the names of all persons buried at the mausoleum. The cards contain date of death, location of burial and possibly other information such as name of spouse, date the burial crypt was sold, who it was sold to, and the mortician handling the burial.

If you believe that a relative is buried at Cypress View Mausoleum, contact them at (619) 264-3168 and they will search their card file for the individuals you request information about. The address of the mausoleum is 3953 Imperial Avenue, San Diego, CA 92113, and they are open 8 a.m. to 5 p.m., seven days a week.

Greenwood Memorial Park
Fred Rimbach writes that "When San Diego was showing early efforts of what was later to be a phenomenal growth, a group of progressive businessmen organized Greenwood Memorial Park. ... The first burial took place on December 17, 1907 ... in Laurel Place."[26] Greenwood Memorial Park is adjacent to Mount Hope on the east. As the cemetery expanded, the office was removed to the eastern end of the cemetery, but the original entrance was adjacent to the front door of Cypress View Mausoleum.

Because of this, the first burials at the cemetery occurred near the old front door to the cemetery in locations like Laurel Place, Hawthorne, Palm Terrace, Arbor Vitale, Magnolia Place and Olive. This cemetery is pleasant to walk around in, and most of the tombstones are similar in appearance because, as Fred Rimbach states: "For uniformity, Greenwood has regulations for plantings and monuments."[27]

Laurie Bissell adds, p. 288, that: "Over the years, development of Greenwood included several chapels, a mortuary, crematory, three mausoleums, a collection of international and rare vegetation, a flower shop, and statuary. Judging by the names of some of the people resting in Greenwood, it must have been attractive from the start. A few of the prominent burials include the Seftons, Scripps, Grants, Putnams, Kettners, Frosts, and Timkens."[28] In fact Ulysses S. Grant, Jr. is buried here, as is Moses Luce, a Civil War Medal of Honor winner.

Many pioneers of San Diego were buried at Greenwood Cemetery, but remember that unless they were removed to Greenwood from other locations, they would have to have died after 1907 when the cemetery was opened. If you believe that a relative is buried at Greenwood Cemetery, call the cemetery office for additional information. Their phone number is (619) 264-3131, and their mailing address is 4300 Imperial Avenue, San Diego, CA 92102. The grounds are fenced. Grounds hours are 8:00 a.m. to dusk, but the records department is only open from 8:00 to around 4:00 p.m.

Holy Cross Catholic Cemetery
Holy Cross Cemetery was dedicated in 1919, and it is the only Catholic cemetery currently in operation in San Diego. As Fred Rimbach states, in his section on Holy Cross: "Holy Cross covers 40 acres. In 1939...the Holy Cross Chapel Mausoleum was built. ... On May 31, 1948, the latest addition to the mausoleum was added, which includes about 2000 more crypts, making a total of 3600 crypts."[29] The oldest sections of Holy Cross Cemetery are the St Bernards, St Pauls, St Josephs and St Francis sections, and again, be aware that your relative, unless they were removed here from another location, would have to have died around 1919 to be buried here.

If you believe that a relative is buried at Holy Cross Cemetery, contact their office for further information. The address is 4470 Hilltop Drive, San Diego, CA 92102. The phone number is (619) 264-3127. Office hours are M-F, 8 a.m. to 4:30 p.m., and Saturday from 9 a.m. to 1 p.m. The grounds are fenced, and are only open from 8 a.m. to 4:30 p.m. The mausoleum is open until 4:00 p.m. daily.

Home of Peace Jewish Cemetery
On p. 272, Laurie Bissell takes up the story of Jewish burials in San Diego that was begun under the heading of "Old Jewish Cemetery" above. Laurie Bissell continues: "Population shifted with time leaving Roseville and the [Old Jewish] cemetery inconveniently far from town. Congregation Beth Israel petitioned the City for land in Mount Hope Cemetery for a Jewish burial ground. They received the land in 1892, establishing the 'Home of Peace' cemetery. With Home of Peace available, the Jewish community discontinued use of the old cemetery.

"In 1937, they reinterred those buried at the Old Jewish Cemetery into Home of Peace, but retained ownership of the land. During World War II they leased the old cemetery land to the Federal Government for a housing project, those homes eventually being replaced by Doctor's (now Sharp Cabrillo) Hospital."[30] A survey has been done of Home of Peace Cemetery and the information has been computerized. Contact the cemetery office below for additional information.

There is also a tombstone book containing Home of Peace tombstone inscriptions entitled *"Tombstone Inscriptions for San Diego, CA"* which is located at the Family History Center. The book contains 30 pages of inscriptions for this cemetery, but the recent survey of the cemetery will probably be more complete. There is a small gate to the right of the main gates at Home of Peace which is open to pedestrian traffic. The main gates are open on a limited basis, but the site is unstaffed.

For further information about burials and hours of operation, contact Home of Peace, 6363 El Cajon Boulevard, San Diego, CA. Their phone number is (619) 286-1867. This cemetery is located at the southwest corner of Mount Hope cemetery with an entrance on Imperial Avenue. The cemetery address is 3668 Imperial Avenue, San Diego, CA 92102.

Fort Rosecrans National Cemetery
The Post Cemetery at Ft. Rosecrans is, as Fred Rimbach writes, "Popularly known as the 'Bennington Cemetery'. [It marks] "...the last resting place of those killed when the American gunboat of that name blew up in San Diego Harbor, July, 1905, killing 60 men. It also contains the bodies of 18 officers and men killed in the Battle of San Pasqual. Rosecrans was established as a post cemetery in June, 1883."[31]

Laurie Bissell, on pp. 277-278, discusses Fort Rosecrans National Cemetery: "Located on Point Loma in an area with a spectacular view of the ocean and San Diego, Fort Rosecrans Cemetery began as part of 1,000 acres set aside for military purposes in 1852. Although Ballast Point is believed to be the location of burials from 1542 and 1602, the first recorded burials in the area began in 1856. Later, a one-acre plot was designated for the use as a burial ground for the Army's San Diego Barrack.

"The cemetery expanded to 10 acres with the 1889 [1899?] dedication of the fort named after General William Starke Rosecrans who died the previous year. His contribution to the United States included military service in the Civil War, as U.S. Minister to Mexico, and as U.S. Congressman from California. ... Servicemen from as far back as the Civil War rest in Fort Rosecrans, including seven Medal of Honor winners--the government's highest award for bravery."[32]

At Fort Rosecrans National Cemetery, there is a computer screen housed in a kiosk outside the cemetery office which can be used to determine if a particular veteran is buried at this cemetery. Also in the kiosk are several ring binders containing alphabetical lists of all veterans buried at Fort Rosecrans, giving the date of internment, rank, and section of the cemetery where the veterans are buried. Many of the tombstones have numbers on the back, and by going to a section and looking at the tombstone numbers, a researcher can find particular tombstones. At times, the name of the veteran's wife is on the back of the tombstone along with her date of death.

Fort Rosecrans National Cemetery is listed in the San Diego phone book under "National Cemetery--Fort Rosecrans." The cemetery is physically located a mile from Cabrillo National Monument on Point Loma. Their mailing address is Fort Rosecrans National Cemetery, P.O. Box 6237 Point Loma, San Diego, CA 92106. Their phone number is (619) 553-2084. Office hours are M-F, 8 a.m. to 4:30 p.m. The fenced grounds are open seven days a week from 8 a.m. to 5 p.m. (8-7 on Memorial Day).

Other Cemeteries in or near San Diego

Glen Abbey Cemetery
This cemetery is located at 3838 Bonita Road, Bonita, CA 91902. Phone: (619) 498-4600. Hours: Office: M-F, 8-5; S-S, 8-4:30; Grounds: 7 a.m. to dusk. It serves the South Bay areas of National City, Chula Vista, Bonita, and Imperial Beach. There is a list of persons buried at Glen Abbey at the Family History Center entitled *"Glen Abbey Cemetery, Chula Vista, California--Tombstone Inscriptions to 1968"*. This large volume contains at least 324 pages of tombstone inscriptions from the cemetery and a 70 page index. Many tombstone inscriptions dating from the late 1800s appear in the Glen Abbey book.

La Vista Memorial Park
This cemetery is located at 3191 Orange Street, National City, CA. Phone: (619) 262-1225. Hours: Office: 8-5, M-F; S-S, by appointment Grounds: 8-5, M-F; S-S, 9-4. This cemetery serves the South Bay area and has been in existence since 1868, making it one of the oldest cemeteries in the area.

There are two books located at the Family History Center which summarize burials at La Vista Cemetery. One is entitled *Tombstone Inscriptions: San Diego and Riverside Counties, CA*. The other book, also for sale by the San Diego Genealogical Society, is entitled *San Diego Cemetery and Burial Records, Vol. 1*, which contains cemetery and burial records for Rancho de la Nation/La Vista Cemetery in National City.

A visit to La Vista Cemetery reveals a fenced, hilly cemetery with a number of tombstones dating from the 1870's. The "Non-Endowment" section of the cemetery contains some of the oldest graves. The Kimball family, founders of National City, are buried here.

El Cajon Cemetery
This is one of the older cemeteries in the San Diego area, and is located at 1270 Pepper Drive, El Cajon, CA 92021. Phone: (619) 442-0052 (Cemetery Office). Hours: Office: M-F, 9-3:30; Grounds--every day: 8 a.m to dusk (5:00 p.m. in winter; 7:30 p.m. in summer). El Cajon Cemetery serves the East County area, including El Cajon, Lakeside and Santee. A three page listing at the Family History Center of individuals buried at El Cajon Cemetery is entitled *"Tombstone Inscriptions, San Diego and Riverside Counties, CA*. A group from San Diego Genealogical Society has also completed transcribing tombstone inscriptions at this cemetery.

El Camino Memorial Park
This cemetery is located at 5600 Carroll Canyon Road, San Diego, CA 92121. Phone: (619) 453-2121. Hours: M-F, 8-5; Grounds: 7:30 a.m. to dusk. The cemetery serves the northern areas of the City of San Diego and is one of the newer cemeteries in the area.

There are other cemeteries in outlying areas of San Diego County which will not be named here. If you wish further information about these cemeteries, check the listings below where additional cemetery books containing tombstone inscriptions are discussed. Also contact the San Diego Historical Society, the California Room of the downtown San Diego Public library, and historical societies in the location you are researching for further information on cemeteries that are of interest to you.

Books Containing Cemetery Information
The following books are available at the Family History Center, the best collection of these types of books in the city. Most of the books feature cemeteries in outlying areas of San Diego, primary in north and east county. The books available at this location include:

Tombstone Inscriptions for San Diego, CA. A listing of tombstone inscriptions for Mount Hope Cemetery (29 pages only, a partial listing of what appears to be the Masonic Section), Home of Peace Jewish Cemetery, (30 pages), Holy Cross Cemetery (several pages), and Calvary Cemetery (30 pages).

Tombstone Inscriptions: San Diego and Riverside Counties, CA. Includes inscriptions for El Camino Memorial Park (9 pages), Jamul Cemetery (2 pages), Miramar Cemetery (2 pages), La Vista Cemetery, partial (12 pages), Mt. Olivet Cemetery in Nestor (5 pages), El Cajon Cemetery (3 pages), Temecula Cemetery (9 pages), Alpine Cemetery (12 pages), plus several small cemeteries (Kolb Cemetery, Higgins Family Cemetery and a small private cemetery), each with 2 pages. This publication is also indexed.

Cemetery Records of San Diego County. Tombstone information from Rancho de la Nacion and Vista Cemeteries (1870-1888), San Pasqual Cemetery tombstone inscriptions compiled in 1981; La Vista Cemetery in National City (records 1881-1890s), Escondido Cemetery records containing birth and death information (1883-1960), and Mount Hope Cemetery ("B" and "C" surname listings only).

Glen Abbey Cemetery, Chula Vista, California: Tombstone Inscriptions to 1968. This 393 page book contains 324 pages of inscriptions from the late 1800s to around 1940 and a 70 pp. index.

Evergreen Park Cemetery. This is a group of miscellaneous records, including burials and an index of burials for Evergreen Park Cemetery, La Mesa, plus internment records from Stokes Funeral Parlor (1911-21) and Erickson Funeral Parlor (1921-1930).

Escondido Cemetery Records 1883-1960. This volume contains about 40 pages of records filed by name and gives birth and death dates.

San Diego County Cemeteries, CA. Includes information from Oceanview (37 pages), Brodie (1 page), Hays Cemeteries (1 page) in Oceanside and San Luis Rey (13 pages), Episcopal All Saints (3 pages) and Freeman Cemeteries (2 pages) at San Luis Rey.

Oceanview Memorial Park Cemetery Records, Oceanside, CA, a few records from this cemetery.

Eternal Hills Cemetery, Oceanside, CA--Tombstone Inscriptions. This volume contains 177 pages of inscriptions and a 40 page index.

Inscriptions and Records of Oceanview Cemetery. Around 100 pages of inscriptions and a 39 page index.

Olivenhain County Cemetery: A Written Record. This contains 14 pages of inscriptions.

Two San Diego Cemeteries. Inscriptions for Julian Cemetery and Deerborn Memorial Park at Poway.

Flynn Springs Cemetery, Lakeside, CA. Two pages of inscriptions.

Evergreen Cemetery, El Centro, CA. This volume is nearly 1,000 pages long and contains tombstone inscriptions from El Centro in Imperial County.

The following cemetery books or articles are available at the San Diego Public Library:

Inventory List of El Campo Santo Cemetery, by the late Lawrence Riveroll-Carrillo.

Confederate Veterans Buried in the United Daughters of the Confederacy Plot at Mt. Hope Cemetery, San Diego, CA, by the United Daughters of the Confederacy.

A History of the Cemeteries in the City of San Diego, California, by Fred Jay Rimbach.

Burying Grounds at Old Town San Diego and Mission Hills, by Orion M. Zink

Vital Records From Cemeteries in California, microfilm. Vol. 11 covers San Diego.

The Civil War Veterans of San Diego, by Barbara Palmer. Contains tombstone inscriptions for nearly 1,000 Civil War veterans and their wives who are buried at Mount Hope Cemetery and several other cemeteries in San Diego. These are nearly all Union veterans, although there are a few Confederate veterans primarily buried at Mount Hope Cemetery. This book will be republished in 2005 by Willow Bend Books at www.WillowBendBooks.com.

San Diego Genealogical Society has these cemetery books: *Mount Hope Cemetery Burial Records, Volume 1, 1869-1909* (Vol. 2 burials are currently featured in their *Leaves & Saplings* newsletter) and *Episcopal Church Records: Holy Trinity Episcopal and St. Pauls Episcopal*, listing 89 burials from 1873-1887. The group recently transcribed tombstones for Alpine Cemetery in east San Diego County.

TAKING YOUR RESEARCH PAST SAN DIEGO

There are several facilities in San Diego which will help you extend your research to other locations throughout the United States, and they will be mentioned briefly here. But first, a word about classes.

If you are interested in extending your study to other locations, take a good basic course in genealogy offered free at the Family History Center in Mission Valley and from North County Genealogical Society. Other classes are held by various organizations for research on the British Isles and for those with German, Scandinavian, Italian, Afro-American, Jewish or Hispanic descent.

Announcements for all classes and genealogy conferences are on the bulletin board at the Family History Center. See also the Computer Genealogy Society of San Diego's website for listings of classes on genealogy at CGSSD.com. Other locations for genealogical research include the following:

San Diego Family History Center

The Family History Center is one of the main resources for conducting research in other states. There are Family History Centers throughout the United States and they all tap into the large collection of genealogical materials at their main library in Salt Lake City which are compiled by the Church of Jesus Christ of Latter Day Saints.

Use of the computers at the Family History Center in Mission Valley is free. There is a nominal charge per page for computer printouts and 25 cents a page for reader/printer printouts of microfilm or microfiche pages. The following indexes or library catalogs are available on Family History Center computers:

Ancestral File Computer Index: By typing in a surname you are researching, you may be able to tap into another person's research, pull up an entire pedigree chart for the individual you are searching, and go several generations or more up your family tree. This is a simple system to use. An instruction book to this computer search program called *FamilySearch: Using Ancestral File* is available at the Family History Center for a nominal charge. These pedigree charts must always be checked for accuracy, however.

International Genealogical Index (IGI) Computer Index: This is a computer list of several hundred million names of deceased persons, and again you can find out information about particular individuals. Pedigree charts cannot be printed out from this source and if that is needed, re-enter the name of your ancestor into the Ancestral File. A small instruction book to this index is called: *FamilySearch: International Genealogical Index*, which can be purchased from the Family History Center for a nominal charge.

Family History Library Catalog: This database lists microfilms and microfiche containing vital records, books, family and local histories and maps that are available at the main Family History Center library in Salt Lake City. The file can be searched by locality or surname. Obtain a microfilm or microfiche number, and you can order the film or fiche from Salt Lake City for a nominal charge. An instruction book on this index is *FamilySearch: Family History Library Catalog* which also can be purchased from the Family History Center for a nominal charge.

The Ancestral File, the library catalog at Salt Lake City, and other information about the Family History Center at Salt Lake City can be accessed online by typing "familysearch" into Google or another Internet search engine. To research a particular ancestor, select "Search" at the top of the screen. When you add the information about your ancestor on the form with blank boxes in it and press "Search" you will come to a selection of persons with similar names and locations where they were born.

Select the name and birth location that most closely fits your ancestor. When you click on that name and get to the listing you selected, see if the word "Pedigree" appears to the far right on the computer screen. If so, click on "Pedigree" to get a pedigree chart with whatever information is available about this ancestor and his parents, grandparents, etc. If you want to see who the individual's children were, click on "Family" and a list of children will come onto the screen.

You can enter your ancestor's name directly into Google or other search engines as someone may have a website devoted to your ancestor. Also, use other free sources on the Internet such as rootsweb to obtain more information about your ancestor.

Carlsbad Library
Another major source is Carlsbad Library, located at 1250 Carlsbad Village Drive (just east of I-5), Carlsbad, CA, 92008. The phone number of the genealogy room is (760) 434-2931 and their hours are M-Th, 9 a.m. to 9 p.m, and F-Sat, 9 a.m. to 5 p.m.

This library has ten or more drawers of microfiche containing family histories, local histories, vital records, and the largest collection of U.S. census index books in the area other than the National Archives in Laguna Niguel, making a trip there a must if you are searching migration patterns of individuals and families through the census indexes. Then come back to San Diego to view the actual census microfilms at the Family History Center in Mission Valley, for they have all census returns for all states and all years from 1790 to 1920 (excluding the 1890 census which was destroyed by fire) and some microfilms from the vast collection of microfilms containing the 1930 census.

Carlsbad library has the largest collection of books on genealogical information in the San Diego area. This library specializes in books and information from other states, and also has a great number of journals and other volumes from all states. You can access Carlsbad library catalog online by typing "Carlsbad Library" into Google or another Internet search engine and clicking on "Catalog".

If you obtain a library card from Carlsbad Library, by using your bar code on the card, you can access HeritageQuest online via your connection online to Carlsbad library. HeritageQuest has the full text of many books of genealogical interest and you may be able to broaden your research considerably by using a free source that would otherwise you cost money to use.

San Diego Public Library--Genealogy Room
The Genealogy Room of the downtown San Diego Public Library is good for researching the eastern states like Massachusetts and for American colonial research. It has the entire series of journals from the New England Historic and Genealogical Society and indexes to those volumes which can be used to locate any ancestors depicted in the journals.

The Genealogy Room has a series of books entitled "Germans in America". These volumes document individual German immigrants who came to the United States from 1850 on. There is a series of books in this collection entitled *The Great Migration Begins*, which list much information about colonial immigrants who came to the American Colonies from 1620 to the mid-1630s.

The Genealogy Room also has Daughters of the American Revolution lineage books and indexes. Look in the indexes to these books to see if your ancestor is listed. If he is, find out which of the lineage books has a listing for him. Go to those lineage books to see if any of the women who have been accepted into the DAR under his name have the same ancestors that you do. If so, you may obtain the lineage papers of these women from the local registrar for the DAR in your area. If you can prove your own personal lineage from a Revolutionary War ancestor, you will, if the proofs are sufficient, be able to join this organization.

Local University Libraries
Local universities have a great deal of information in their libraries not only about San Diego but also about other cities, states and nations. I have researched books on Chicago and other locations in Illinois at the University of California San Diego, for example. This university also has some of the Victoria County Histories which are useful for the study of old English manor houses and their inhabitants.

San Diego State University has a great many local history books from all over the country, and San Diego State University and the University of San Diego are good sources for many theses on famous San Diegans, local architecture, and archeological projects that were conducted in San Diego. You can check the Internet to determine if the catalogues of these libraries are online.

The National Archives at Laguna Niguel
Last but not least is a branch of the National Archives, which is located at 24000 Avila Road, East Laguna Niguel, CA 92677. Their phone number is (949) 360-2611, and their hours are 8-4:30, M-F, and 8-8:30, first Tuesdays of the month, except Federal holidays. Internet address is www.nara.gov, and the e-mail address is archives@laguna.nara.gov. The best times to access records at this facility are in the early morning hours when there is not a line to use the microfilm reader/printers. There is a restaurant in the building which is open to the public. A booklet entitled "Index to Microfilms in the Research Room" can be also obtained by calling (949) 360-2641.

This facility has a great many bound volumes of census indexes which will be useful in locating ancestors in states and towns from 1790 through 1900. The census indexes for various states will give the names of individuals, their residence location, and the page number upon which their name appears for that residence location. An example in the 1790 census book for Massachusetts might be: "Brown, John Bost:243" and you feel that this is your ancestor.

Once you find your ancestor's residence location and the page number on which he appears in the 1790 census for Boston, go to the Family History Center in Mission Valley which has census microfilms for all states and all census years through 1920, with some microfilms of the 1930 census. Locate the census microfilm for Massachusetts for 1790, go to the Boston listings on that microfilm, and then go to p. 243, where you will find your ancestor listed.

Please be aware that only heads of households were listed on the census enumerations from 1790 to 1840; it was not until the 1850 census that wives and children were also listed on the census.

The National Archives also has all the Soundex indexes on microfilm. Soundex is a system used to index names that sounded alike for the 1900, 1910 and 1920 census years for families with children. The Soundex indexes help to identify the Enumeration District that your ancestor appears in for these census years, for you must know the Enumeration District your ancestor lived in in large cities in order to find your ancestors on the census microfilms for those cities. Knowing the Enumeration District that your ancestor lived and the page number upon which your ancestor appears in saves you the trouble of going through the census page by page to find a listing for your ancestor in the larger cities.

There are also indexes available on microfilm at Laguna Niguel in which you can obtain a pension file number for a Revolutionary War ancestor, just as you did for the Civil War ancestor discussed in "Military Records" above. Then, order the Revolutionary War ancestor's file from the National Archives in Washington, D.C. using NAFT Form 80. A sampling of other microfilms available at Laguna Niguel includes:

Index to Compiled Service Records of Confederate Soldiers, microfilm M253 V9

Index to Compiled Service Records of Volunteer Union Soldiers, various microfilms, V9-11

Index to Compiled Service Records of Union Colored Troops, M589 V11

Special Census Enumerating Veterans & Widows of the Civil War, 1890, M123 11

Headstone Records for Civil War Union and some 1812 Veterans, 1879-1938, M1845 V12

Registers of the Pacific Branch, Sawtelle Home for Disabled Soldiers, 1882-1938, M1749 V12

Burial Registers for Military Posts, Camps and Sections 1768-1921, M2014 V12

Army Post Returns for California and Arizona, 1800-1916, M617 V12

Again, the National Archives is good for census indexes, for indexes to the service record numbers for veterans, and for other microfilms containing information as described in the booklets mentioned above. It is also not far from the Carlsbad library, and if you cannot find a particular census index for a state you are researching, drop down to the Carlsbad library, which may have that index.

CONCLUSION

As you can see, there is a wealth of genealogical information available for researchers in and around San Diego and the only requirement is to get out there and find out what the records hold for you. I wish you well in your research, and hope that this book will be of use to you on your journey.

INDEX TO HISTORICAL NAMES

INDEX TO HISTORICAL NAMES

This is an alphabetical index of names which appear in the current version of *Family History Research in San Diego*, published in 2005. The index lists only those who played a part in San Diego history, individuals or families who are named in old newspaper obituaries, cemetery records, or other genealogical sources. The list includes the following:

Abbey, Eunice--39
Abbott, Mrs. A.E.--39
Ables, S.E.--60
Adams, Juan--51
Adams, R.--53
Aguilar Family--12
Aguilar, Blas--14
Aguilar, Francisco Javier--8
Aguilar, Rosario--14
Aguirre Family--15,51
Aguirre, Jose Antonio--14,15,47
Alanis Family--12,31
Alanis, Maximo--12
Alden, John--19
Alipas, Damasio--14,16,18
Alipas, Gervasio--14
Alipas, Josefa--18
Alipas, Maria Arcadia--18
Alipas, Ramona--18
Allen, _____--53
Allen, John--33
Altamirano Family--14,15
Altamirano, Jose Antonio--14
Alvarado Family--12,14,15,19
Alvarado, Bernardino de--8
Alvarado, Estefana--17
Alvarado, Francisco Maria--14,17
Alvarado, Jose Maria--47
Alvarado, Juan Bautista de--8,14,16
Alvarado, Maria Antonia--16,18,36
Alvarez Family--12,31
Alvarez, Pedro--9,12
Alvitre, Sebastian de--8
Amador Family--12
Amador, Pedro Antonio--8,17
Ames Family--14,60
Ames, Anne (Mrs. Samuel Ames)--56,58
Ames, Frank--47,54,56,58
Ames, Julian--19
Ames, Samuel--56,58
Arballo, Maria Feliciana--12,16,17
Arce Family--9,12
Arce, Jose Gabriel de--8
Arce, Sebastian Constantino de--8
Arguello Family--13,14
Arguello, Jose Dario--13,18
Arguello, Jose Ramon--14
Arguello, Maria Antonia Lugarda Eufemia--18
Arguello, Maria del Refugio--15,17
Arguello, Maria del Refugio Concepcion--18

Arguello, Santiago--13,14,18
Arguello, Santiago E.--14,47
Arroyo, Josef Manuel--45,50
Badiola, Manuel Antonio--8
Baker, Charlotte--22
Baker, Robert S.--15,16
Ball (Wilder), Peter V.--19
Bandini Family--4,13,15,19,51,60
Bandini, Maria Arcadia--15,16,17
Bandini, Juan--13,14,15,16,17,54
Bandini, Jose--13
Bandini, Maria del Refugio--15
Bandini, Maria Dolores Caledonia--17
Bandini, Maria Ysidora Barbara--17
Baranceanu, Belle--22
Barkely, J.T.--49
Barnett, Mrs.--59
Barona (Varona), Fr. Josef--36
Baxter, E.--58
Bean, Joshua H.--19,54
Bejarano (Vegerano), Jose Maria--8
Bell, Eva (daughter of G.W.)--58
Bell, G.W.--58
Bell, Mrs. G.W. (Nancy Cofer)--58
Bellou, Walter C.--22
Benno, Juan Evangelista--8
Bergman, Jacob--33
Blackmer, Eli T.--33
Bliss, Robert S.--52
Bogart, J.C.--19
Bouchard, Hypoloyte--10
Boyd, John M.--58
Boyd, Mrs. John M. (Addie S.)--58
Boyd, (daughter of John M.)--58
Bradley, R.--53
Brewster, Eliz.--33
Brown, Ana (Mrs. John Huntington)--19
Brown, John F.--17
Brundage, Rebecca (Mrs. William Minter)--19
Burks, Charles M.--33
Burns, Diego (James)--50
Burton, Maria--33
Burton, Maria Amparo de Ruiz--22
Bush, Thomas Henry--19
Bustamante, Manuel--12
Caballero, Fr. Felix--37
Camacho, Jose Anastasio--8
Campbell, Sarah (Mrs. Constantine O'Neill)--19
Caniz, Mr. _____--53
Canizares, Jose de--8

Carmichael, H.C.--49
Carr, Mrs. Celia L.--59
Carrillo Family--12,11,12,13,19
Carrillo, Domingo--14
Carrillo, Guillermo--8,11,45
Carrillo, Isabel--11
Carrillo, Joaquin--11,12,13,14,16
Carrillo, Jose Antonio--14
Carrillo, Joseph Raymundo--9,11,12,14,45,50
Carrillo, Maria Antonia--11,17
Carrillo, Maria Josefa--13,16,20
Carrillo, Maria Ygnacia--11
Carrillo, Mariano--8,11
Carson, Mrs. William (Clara Flynn (Pendleton)--17
Cart, J.--53
Cassidy, Andrew--18,19
Cassidy, Catalina--18
Cassidy, Marcus--18
Castelo, Agustin--8
Chauncey, Emily (Mrs. Benjamin Hayes)--18
Chetwood, Hobart--37
Child, Mr. _____--52
Clayton, Henry--16,18,19
Cline (infant)--60
Cofer, Nancy (Mrs. G.W. Bell)--58
Cole, Augusta (Mrs. Samuel Hackett)--19
Collins, Isaac--57
Condon, John--50
Confer, Alfred--33
Conklin, Norman--38
Connors Family--14
Connors, James W.--19
Connors, Paul--19
Coronel, Juan Antonio--8,21
Corwin, Samuel D.--52
Cota Family--9,12,14
Cota Andres de--8
Cota Pablo Antonio de--8
Cota Roque Jacinto de--12
Couts Family--14,17,60
Couts, Cave Johnson-- 3,14,16,17,18,19,
   22,30,47,51,54
Couts, Wiley Blount--18
Couts, William--17
Couts, Mrs. William (Nancy Johnson)--17
Craft, Delarau--33
Crespi, Fr. Juan--8
Crosthwaite, Philip--17,19,22
Cuero, Delfina--5
Cullin, James W.--55
Curley, William--18,19
Curry, John--57
Daley, Thomas--24
Damschroeder, Clarence--22
Daniels, James--57
Darnell, Thomas R.--19

Davis, Edward Heath--22
Davis, William Heath--25,54
De Camp, Jas. C.--52
De Camp, Mrs. Jas. C. (Ellen)--52
De Camp, John--52
Dehne, Raymond W.--59
Delano, Sally (Mrs. Beriah Fitch)--16
Denny, Joseph--50
Dexter, Lyford L.--48
Dodson, Mrs.--55
Dominguez Family--9,12,13,14
Dominguez, Cristobal--8,12,13,14,15,17,45
Dominguez, Juan Jose--8,13
Dominguez, Maria Francisca Marcelina--15
Dominguez, Maria Victoria--13,47
Donahoe, Henry (son of James)--57
Donahoe, James--57
Drew, Margaret (Mrs. Solomon Stewart)--19
Dunham, Albert Warren--52
Dvorak, Dorothy (Mrs. John Ridington (Wrightington)--19
Dyer, H.C.--57
Dyer, Julia Frances (Mrs. H.C. Dyer)--57
Earle, Louise (Mrs. B. (Bernard?) Etcheverry)--37
Earle, Sophie (Mrs. Peter Remondino)--37
Echeandia, Jose Maria--14,17
Edmonds, Lydia (Mrs. Jesse Hunter)--52
Effinger, Robert Patterson--22
Eisen, George--58
Emell, Frederick--57
England, William J.--33
Ensworth, Augustus S.--19,58,59
Espinosa Family--19
Espinoza, Jose Joaquin--8
Esteban, Fr. Pedro--36
Estudillo Family--4,13,14,15,19,51
Estudillo, Jose Antonio--8,13,14,47
Estudillo, Jose Guadalupe--14
Estudillo, Jose Maria--13,14,17,45,50
Estudillo, Maria Concepcion--17
Estudillo, Maria Dolores Damiana--13,16
Etcheverry, B. (Bernard?)--37
Etcheverry, Mrs. B. (Bernard?) (Louise Earle)--37
Evans, A.W.--48
Evans, William--55
Feliz Family--12,31
Feliz, Vicente--12
Ferrell, William C.--19
Figuer, Fr. Juan--36
Finlie, W.F.--57
Finlie, Mrs. W.F. (Augusta W. Pettit)--57
Finlie, Willie (son of W.F. Finlie)--57
Fischer, Gustave--56
Fischer, Sophia--56
Fitch Family--16
Fitch, Beriah--16

Fitch, Mrs. Beriah (Sally Delano)--16
Fitch, Henry Delano--13,16,18,19,20,22,45,47,49,50
Fitch, Natalia--16,45,50
Flanagan, Mary--52
Flynn, Clara (Pendleton) (Mrs. William Carson--17
Forster, John--16,19,22
Foss, Ed A.--33
Fox, Thomas--58
Franklin, Lewis A.--19
Franklin, Maurice--20
Freeman, Richard--21
Frost Family--63
Fuster, Fr. Vicente--7,36
Gale, William Alden--15,19
Garcia, Fr. Jose--36
Gibson, Isaac M.--53
Gil Family--31
Gitchell, J.R.--19
Givelin, John--57
Gongora, Jose Maria de--8
Gonzalez, Alejo Antonio--8,45
Goodbody, Bernard--49
Gore, Albert--33
Grant Family--63
Grant, Ulysses S., Jr.--63
Gray, Andrew--19
Green, Henry--60
Green, William--56
Griffin, John S.--52
Grijalva, Pablo de--9,45
Groom, Robert W.--19
Gunn Family--4
Gutierrez, Josef--12,16
Gutierrez, Maria Eustaquia--12
Gutierrez, Maria Thomasa--12
Hackett, Samuel--19
Hackett, Mrs. Samuel (Augusta Cole)--19
Hackett, Samuel Warren--19
Haight, John--57
Hall, Hiram S.--33
Hamilton, Martin--33
Hammil, Samuel Wood--22
Harrell, Hiram--33
Hayes, Benjamin F.--16,18,22,38
Hayes, Mrs. Benjamin (Emily Chauncey)--18
Hayes, Mrs. Benjamin (Adelaida Serrano)--18
Hayes, John (father of Benjamin)--18
Hayes, Mrs. John (Maria Simmons)--18
Hayes, John--19
Hayes, William--50
Haywood, Robert E.--33
Hazard, Roscoe--38
Hebbard, William Sterling--22,38
Heintzelman, Samuel P.--22
Higgins Family--65
Higuera, Jose Ignacio de la--8

Hinton, Francis (Jack) (aka Abraham Ten Eyck De Witt Hornbeck)--47,54,56,58
Hoffman, Chauncey--19
Hoffman, David Bancroft--19,38
Hoffman, Eugene--22
Hoffman, Mary--19
Holbein, Fr.--35
Hooper, George--56
Horcasitas, Gertrudis--13
Horton, Alonzo Ebenezer--3,7,14,22,24,61
Howes, _____--53
Howland, John--16
Huff, Karen--22
Huick (Heuck,Heuce), Henrietta--55
Hunter, Diego--52
Hunter, Jesse--52
Hunter, Mrs. Jesse (Lydia Edmonds)--52
Huntington, John--19
Huntington, Mrs. John (Ana Brown)--19
Huntington, Platt--19
Huxford, Thomas L.--50
Hyer, Frederick--50
Ibarra (Ybarra) Family--12,31
Ibarra (Ybarra), Juan Antonio--9,12,16
Ibarra (Ybarra), Maria Angeles--16
Ignacio--8
Indian Joe--6
Israel, Joseph (son of Robert Israel)--57
Israel, Joseph--18
Israel, Mrs. Joseph (Anne Wilson)--18
Israel, Robert DeCatur--18,19,22,57
Jacobs, Mark--20
Jacobs, Victoria--20
Jaume, Fr. Luis--45,50
Johnson, Beannois--17
Johnson, Mrs. Beannois (Abigail Robinson)--17
Johnson, Charles Robinson--17
Johnson, Curtis--33
Johnson, George Alonzo--17,19
Johnson, Henry--50
Johnson, Nancy (Mrs. William Couts)--17
Julian, J.M.--51
Kearney, Lawrence--50
Kelly Family--56
Kelly, Robert--19,56
Kerren, Richard--22,47,50
Kettner Family--63
Kettner, Marion--22
Kettner, William--22
Kimball Family--65
Kimball, Frank--22
Klauber, A.L.--59,60
Klauber, A.L. (infant dau. of)--59
Kurtz, Daniel Brown--19
Ladd, H.C.--56
Ladd, Mrs. H.C. (Sarah R.)--56

Ladd, Phoebe--57
Lasuen, Fr. Fermin Francisco de--7,36
Lazaros, Fr. Nicholas--36
Le Batt, Segemund--59
Lee, J.A.--58
Lee, John--55
Leiva Family--12,31
Leiva, Jose Antonio Ruiz--12
Light, Alan--21
Lindsey, Henry--52
Lisalde Family--12,31
Lisalde, Pedro Antonio--9,12
Little James Henry--58
Lopez Family--12,14,19,31
Lopez, Bonifacio--14,17,47
Lopez, Juan Francisco--9,12,17,45
Lopez, Maria Ignacia Candelaria--13
Lopez, Maria Josefa--17
Lopez, Maria Juliana Josefa--12
Lorenzana Surname--10
Lorenzana, Apolinaria--14
Louis, Isador--20
Lubin, Sigmund--22
Lucas, Tom--6
Luce, Moses--63
Lyons, Andrew--47
Lyons, George--17,19
Machado Family--12,13,14,18,19
Machado-Silvas Family--4,15
Machado-Stewart Family--4,15
Machado-Wrightington Family--15
Machado, Jose Manuel--18,45
Machado, Joseph Manuel--13,14,16,18
Machado, Juana de Dios--16,18,19
Machado, Maria Antonia Juliana--18,19
Machado, Maria Guadalupe Ildefonsa--18,19
Machado, Rose Maria--18,19
Magon, Ricardo Flores--22
Magruder, John Bankhead--22
Malley, Michael--50
Mannasse, Heyman--20
Mannasse, Jacob--47,59
Mannasse, Joseph S.--19,59,60
Mannasse, Moses--47
Manriquez, Sebastian--8,21
Marchant, G.W.--57
Mariner, Fr. Juan--36
Marquez, Maria del Rosario--45
Marron Family--12,13,56
Marron, Juan Maria, Jr.--13,14,47
Marron, Juan Maria, Sr.--13
Marron Sylvester--14
Marshall, Betty (Mrs. Henry Smith)--19
Marston Family--4
Marston, George Phillips--47
Marston, George White--22,38

Martin, Fr. Fernando--37
Martinez, James--6
Masaharu, Kondo--21
McClullen, Neil--53
McCoy, James--19,58
Menendez, Fr. Antonio--14,37
Merkley, H.W.--49
Miles, John F.--33
Mill, Anson Peaslee--22
Miller, ____--53
Minter, John--19
Minter, William--19
Minter, Mrs. William (Rebecca Brundage)--19
Miranda, Juan Maria--8
Monroy Family--31
Moon, William H.--19,57
Morillo Family--12
Morse, Ephraim Weed--19,22,56
Morse, Lydia A.--56
Mortenson, John--22
Nagle, Patrick--50
Newburger, Ike--59
Newlands, James--50
Nieto Family--12
Nieto, Jose Manuel Perez--12
Nieto, Juan Crispin Perez--12
Nieto, Manuel--9
Noell, Charles P.--19
Noriega, Jose Antonio Guerrera y--14
Noyes, William H.--19
Ochoa, Francisco Javier--8
Ojeda, Jose Gabriel de--8
Oliva, Fr. Vicente Pascual--7,37
Olivera Family--12,31
Olivera, Juan Maria--12
Olvera, Agustin--17
O'Neill, Constantine--19
O'Neill, Mrs. Constantine (Sarah Campbell)--19
O'Neill, Patrick--19,47
Ortega Family--9,11,12,31
Ortega, Jose Francisco de--8,11,13,17
Ortega, Juan de--7
Ortega, Maria del Pilar--13
Ortega, Maria del Refugio de Jesus--17
O'Sullivan, Jeremiah--50
Osuna Family--9,12,13,51
Osuna, Juan Ismerio de--8,12
Osuna, Juan Luis de--8
Osuna, Juan Maria--12,13,14,47
Osuna, Leandro--14
Osuna, Maria Felipa--13
Osuna, Ramon--14
Painter, Frederick J.--56
Palmer Family--5
Panto, Jose--6
Panto, Fr. Pedro--36

Parker, Edwin--38
Parker, Walter--33
Pattie, Sylvester--50
Paycras, Fr. Mariano--36
Pearne, Thomas H. (child of)--52
Pedrorena Family--14,15,51
Pedrorena, Maria Antonia de--47
Pedrorena, Miguel de--14
Pena Family--12
Pendleton, Eugene--17
Pendleton, George Allan--17,19,47,55
Peters, John (son of John)--18
Peters, John--18
Peters, Mrs. John (Josefina)--18
Pettit, Augusta W. (Mrs. W.F. Finlie)--57
Pickering, Thomas L.--56
Pico Family--12,14,19,31
Pico (Pio) Family--14
Pico, Andres--12,14,16,47
Pico, Jose Antonio Bernardo--14,47
Pico, Jose Maria--9,12,14
Pico, Maria Isadora Ygnacia--16
Pico, Maria Tomasa--14,17
Pico, Pio--12,14,16,47
Pico, Santiago de la Cruz--9,12,16
Polock, Lewis--20
Poole, Charles Henry--19
Portola, Gaspar de--8
Putnam Family--63
Quale, Edward--22,38
Questin, Isabel (Mrs. Charles Wilder)--19
Quin, Ah--20,21,22
Reid Brothers (architects)--22,38
Remondino, Peter Charles--22,37
Remondino, Mrs. Peter (Sophie Earle)--37
Requa, Richard--22,38
Reyes, Martin--8
Reyes-Ybanez, Maria--8,13,15
Rice, Lillian Jenette--22,38
Richil, Henry V.--33
Ridington (Wrightington), John--19
Ridington (Wrightington), Mrs. John (Dorothy Dvorak)--19
Ridington (Wrightington), Thomas--16,19
Rios, Feliciano--9
Ritchey, Bert--21
Rivera y Moncada, Fernando Javier de--8,9
Rivera, Joseph Maria--7
Rivera, Mariana--7
Rivera, Simon Maria (son of Joseph Maria Rivera)--7
Roberts, Lyman--33
Robinson, Abigail (Mrs. Beannois Johnson)--17
Robinson, Alfred--15
Robinson, James W.--19
Robles, Juan Jose de--8
Rocha, Juan Jose--14

Rodriguez Family--12
Rodgiguez, Juan--14
Rodriguez, Juana Maria Simona--12
Rodriguez, Maria Lucinda--12
Rodriguez, Vicente Villa--12
Roger, Thomas--50
Rogers, Malcom J.--22
Romero Family--31
Romero, Felipe--9,12,45
Romero-Garcia, Petra--45
Rosas Family--12,31
Rose, Louis--19,20,59
Rosecrans, William Starke--64
Ross, Michael--50
Rourke, Anne Jane--58
Rourke, J.--58
Rubio Family--12,31
Rubio, Bernardo--8
Rubio, Jose Carlos--8
Rubio, Mateo--9,12
Ruiz Family--11
Ruiz, Antonio Vicente--8
Ruiz, Francisco Maria--11,12,14
Ruiz, Ignacio--9,13
Ruiz, Juan Maria--11
Ruiz, Maria de la Luz--13
Russel, Joseph Warren--57
Russell, Eugene--52
Russell, Thomas--16
Sanchez, Fr. Josef--36
Sandey, Mary Jane--53
Sandey, William A.--53
Sautill, Mr. [Amos?]--53
Savin, Adolphis--54
Sawtell, Amos--52,53
Sawyer, J.A.--53
Schiller, Marcus--19,20,59
Scripps Family--63
Scripps, Edward Willis--22
Scripps, Ellen Browning--22
Sefton Family--63
Seeley, A.L. (child of)--55
Seeley, Albert--55
Seeley, Mrs. Albert (Emily Walker)--55
Seeley, Cecilia--55
Seeley, Florence--55
Sepulveda Family--31
Sepulveda, Francisco Xavier--9
Serra, Fr. Junpero--8
Serrano Family--14,19
Serrano, Adelaida (Mrs. Benjamin Hayes)--18
Serrano, Francisco--9,18,45
Serrano, Jose Antonio--14
Serrano, Rafaela--14
Serrano, Rosa--18
Shaffer, Bernard--59

Shaw, F.M.--57
Shaw, Mrs. F.M. (Lizzie M.)--57
Shearer, Judge--57
Shearer, S., (son of Judge Shearer)--57
Sherman, Augusta--61
Sherman, Matthew--61
Silvas Family--12,31
Silvas, Ana Maria Gertrudis--12
Silvas, Jose Antonio Nicasio--19
Silvas, Jose Miguel--9,45
Silvas, Joseph Manuel--9,12,45
Silvas, Lorenza--19
Silvas, Maria Balbaneda--12,18
Silvas, Maria Bernarda--12
Silvas, Maria Josefa Gabriela--12
Simmons, Maria (Mrs. John Hayes)--18
Simpson, Matthew--53
Sinusin, Clara--12
Sloane, Joshua--19
Smith, Albert Benjamin--19,47
Smith, Alexander--33
Smith, George--19
Smith, Henry--19
Smith, Mrs. Henry (Betty Marshall)--19
Smith, Maria Providencia--18,19
Smith, William--50
Snook, Joseph Francis--16,45,50
Soberanes, Joseph Maria--9
Sotelo Family--12,31
Sotelo, Francisco--12
Soto (Sotomayor), Alejandro--8
Soto, Ignacio--9
Soto, Lorenzo--47
Soto, Mateo Ignacio de--8
Stearns Family--13,16
Stearns, Abel--13,15,16
Steele, Francis--54,56
Steiner, Sig--20
Stewart, John Collins--19
Stewart, Maria Nieves--19
Stewart, Solomon Freeman--19
Stewart, Mrs. Solomon Freeman (Margaret Drew)--19
Stokes, E.H.--49
Stokes, Edward--17
Streeter, Mr. ____--52
Sutherland, Thomas W.--19
Sweeney, Thomas W.--22
Taggart, Charles--47
Tarabal, Sebastian--8
Tebbitts, George P.--19
Tellec, Martin--33
Timken Family--63
Tolman, George B.--57
Tolman, George P. (son of George B. Tolman)--57
Torrent, Fr. Hilario--36
Trasvina, Antonio--8

Turner, Nicholas--53
Tyler, ____--53
Ubach, Fr. Antonio--14,44,60
Urselino, Josef--45
Utt, Levi H.--33
Valdes, Juan Bautista--8
Valdes, Maria Serafina--13,16,18
Valenzuela Family--12,31
Valenzuela, Juan--12
Valenzuela, Maria del Carmen--18
Valenzuela, Maria Gorgona--13
Valesch, William--52
Varona (Barona), Fr. Josef--36
Vastida, Maria Jacinta--16
Vegerano (Bejarano), Jose Maria--8
Velasquez, Jose--8
Velasquez, Maria de los Angeles--16
Venegas, Susana--17
Verdugo Family--11,12,31
Verdugo, Jose Maria--11
Verdugo, Juan Diego--11
Verdugo, Juan Maria--11
Verdugo, Mariano--8,11
Verdugo, Narciso--8
Verdugo, Ygnacio Leonardo--11
Verduzco, Anastasio--8
Verlaque, Theophile--22
Villalobo Family--12
Villar(d) Family--17,19
Villard, Bernarda--17
Villard, Francisco--17
Villard, Martina--17
Viscaino, Sebastian--22
Walker, Emily (Mrs. Albert Seeley)--55
Walker, Mary--21
Wall, Enos A.--19
Ward, Sampson--33
Warner, Jonathan T. (Trumbell)--19
Warren, Richard--16,19
Waterman, Hazel Wood--22,38
Waterman, Robert Whitney--22
Watson, Charles C.--33
Weddle, H.H.--58
Weddle, Mary Ellen (dau. W.H. Weddle)--58
Weighorst, Olaf--22
Whaley, Anna E. (Lannay)--55
Whaley, Thomas--19,22,54,55,58
Whaley, Tommie--54,58
Whipple, Amiel Weeks--22
Whitney, Willard--33
Whitson, W.W.--48
Wilcox, Alfred--18
Wilcox, Alfred Henry--17,18
Wilcox, Mary--18
Wilder, Charles--19
Wilder, Mrs. Charles (Isabel Questin)--19

Wilder, Maria Dolores--19
Wilder, Maria Refugia--19
Wilder (Ball), Peter V.--19
William, Charles--22
Williams, George--50
Williams, William ("Cockney Bill")--18
Wilson, Anne (Mrs. Joseph Israel)--18
Wilson, Bob--22
Wilson, Don Benito--22
Witherby, Oliver S.--19,22,38
Woodbey, George Washington--22
Wrightington (Ridington), John--19
Wrightington (Ridington), Mrs. John (Dorothy Dvorak)--19
Wrightington, Maria Serafina--19
Wrightington (Ridington), Thomas--16,19
Wuest, Albert--24
Ybarra (Ibarra) Family--12,31
Ybarra (Ibarra), Juan Antonio--9,12,16
Ybarra (Ibarra), Maria Angeles--16
Yorba Family--9,12,31
Yorba, Antonio--8,9,12,16
Yorba, Maria Raymunda Fermina--16
Young, John N.--48
Zamarano, Augustin V.--14
Zuniga Family--31

CITATIONS AND IMAGE SOURCES

CITATIONS AND IMAGE SOURCES

Citations

1. R. Clinton Griffin, *Mission San Diego de Alcala Baptisms 1769-1799*, (San Diego, CA: R. Clinton Griffin, 1999), p. 36.

2. Ibid.

3. R. Clinton Griffin, *Mission Basilica San Diego de Alcala: Burials for Mission and Presidio 1775-1831*, (San Diego, CA: R. Clinton Griffin, 1999), p. 6.

4. R. Clinton Griffin, *El Campo Santo [The Holy Field] San Diego, California: Burials 1849-1880*, (San Diego, CA: R. Clinton Griffin, 1998), p. 40.

5. William Mason, *The Census of 1790: A Demographic History of Colonial California*, (Novato, CA: Ballena Press, 1998, pp. 40-41, 44.

6. Ibid, p. 114.

7. William Mason, "The Garrisons of San Diego Presidio: 1770-1794," *Journal of San Diego History*, Vol. XXIV, No. 4, (Fall 1978), p. 420.

8. Winifred Davidson, "Henry Fitch's grave inscription, note of Judge Benjamin Hayes in 1873, from the unpublished diary, notes, letters of Judge Hayes in Cave Couts' possession--Winifred Davidson's 1932 notes", San Diego Historical Society.

9. Betsy Green, *Discovering the History of Your House and Your Neighborhood*, (Santa Monica, CA: Santa Monica Press, 2002), pp. 63-64.

10. Laurie Bissell, "San Diego Cemeteries: A Brief Guide", *Journal of San Diego History*, Vol. XXVIII (Fall 1982), p. 270.

11. Fred Rimbach, Jr., "A History of the Cemeteries of the City of San Diego, California", (San Diego, CA: Fred Jay Rimbach, Jr., 1949), at the downtown San Diego Public Library, California Room, unnumbered pages relating to Presidio Hill cemetery.

12. Ibid, Bissell, p. 271.

13. William Smythe, *History of San Diego*, (San Diego, CA: The History Company, 1908), p. 242.

14. Dr. John S. Griffin, *A Doctor Comes to California: The Diary of John S. Griffin, Assistant Surgeon with Kearny's Dragoons, 1846-1847*, (San Francisco, CA: California Historical Society, MCMXLIII), pp. 74, 76, copy at the San Diego Historical Society.

15. Robert S. Bliss, "Diary of Robert S. Bliss, Company 'B' Mormon Battalion, U.S. Army, 1846-1847", pp. 18, 19, copy at the San Diego Historical Society.

16. James E. Kirby, "Matthew Simpson's Diary: A Wednesday in San Diego, 1854," *Journal of San Diego History*, Vol. XXIX, No. 3, (Summer 1983), pp. 222-223.

17. Ibid, Bissell, p. 271-272.

18. Tombstone inscription for Frank Ames, from an article in the June 29, 1975 *San Diego Union*.

Citations and Image Sources, p. 2

Citations (con't)

19. Letter of Squire Augustus S. Ensworth to Thomas Whaley, May 21, 1862, archives of Old Town San Diego State Historic Park.

20. Ibid, Letter from Ensworth to Whaley, September 12, 1861.

21. Ibid, Bissell, p. 272.

22. Orion Zink, *Burying Grounds at Old Town San Diego and Mission Hills*, manuscript at downtown San Diego Public Library, California Room, unnumbered pages relating to Old Jewish Cemetery.

23. Ibid, Bissell, p. 276.

24. Ibid.

25. Brae Canlen, "Tombstone Territory: The Business of Burial at Mount Hope Cemetery," *San Diego Weekly Reader*, April 7, 1988.

26. Ibid, Rimbach, unnumbered pages relating to Greenwood Memorial Park.

27. Ibid.

28. Ibid, Bissell, p. 288.

29. Ibid, Rimbach, unnumbered pages relating to Holy Cross Catholic Cemetery.

30. Ibid, Bissell, p. 272.

31. Ibid, Rimbach, unnumbered pages relating to Fort Rosecrans National Cemetery.

32. Ibid, Bissell, pp. 277-278.

Image Sources

The author wishes to thank the following individuals for permission to reproduce cemetery maps in this publication: David Lugo, Cemetery Manager, Calvary and Mount Hope Cemeteries of the City of San Diego; Mauricio Perez, Manager, Cypress View Mausoleum; Mario De Blasio, General Manager, Holy Cross Cemetery; and Bill Livingston, Director, Fort Rosecrans National Cemetery. The map of San Diego in 1873 is presented courtesy of the National Archives, Washington, D.C.

MAP OF SAN DIEGO (1873) AND SOME CEMETERY MAPS

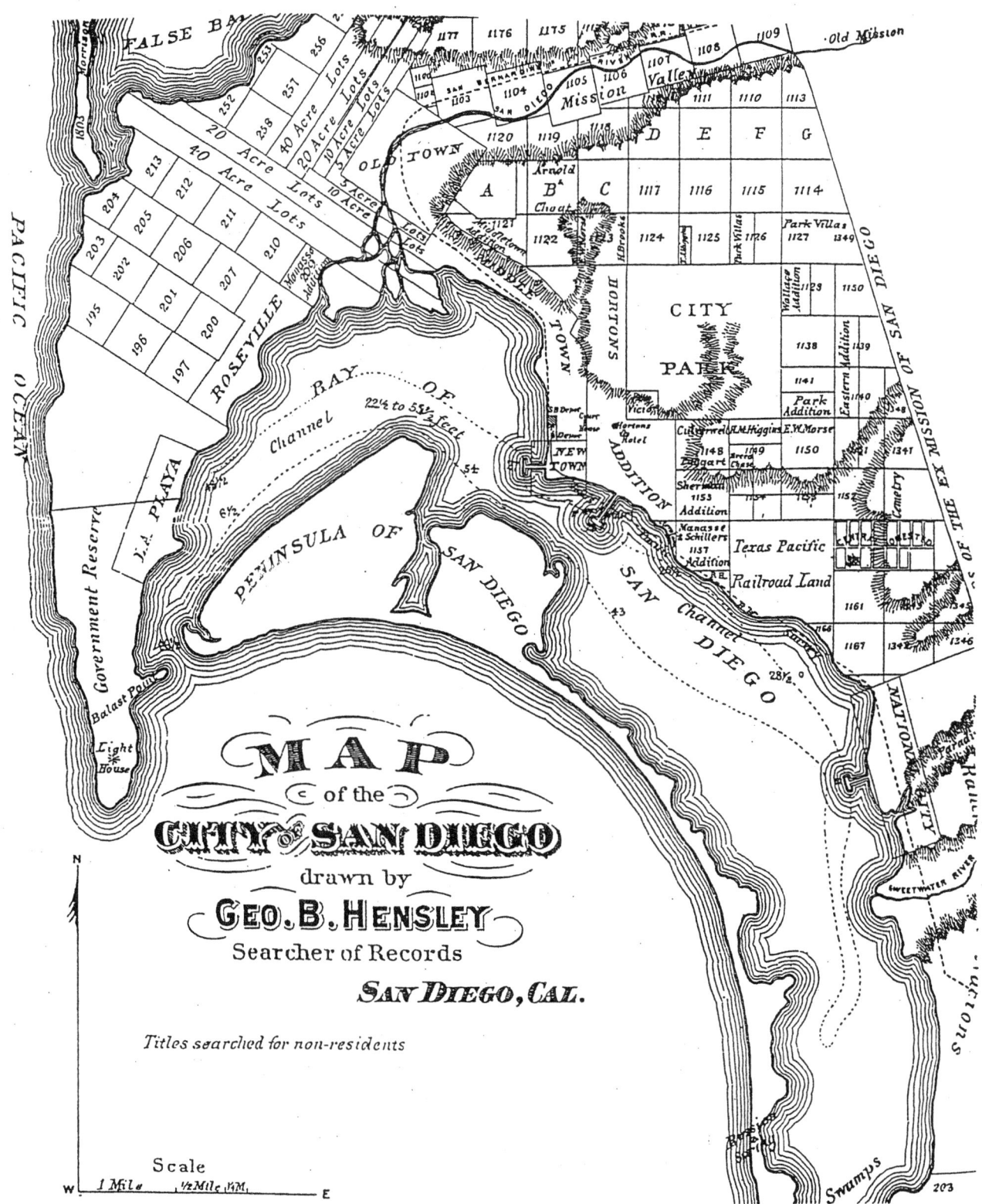

MAP OF SAN DIEGO IN 1873

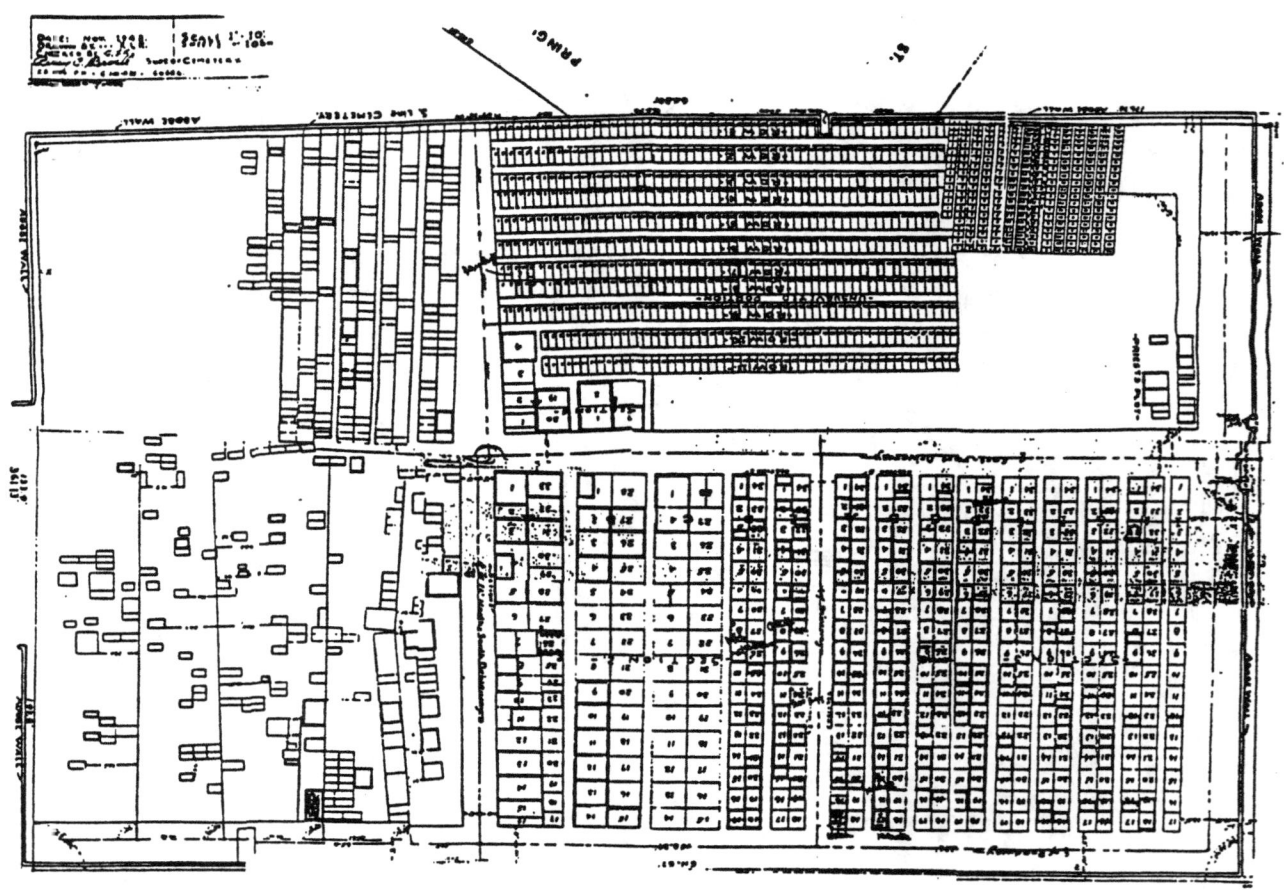

Note: Map, reversed to show street side at bottom, causes grave numbers and map lettering to be upside down

CALVARY (MISSION HILLS) CEMETERY

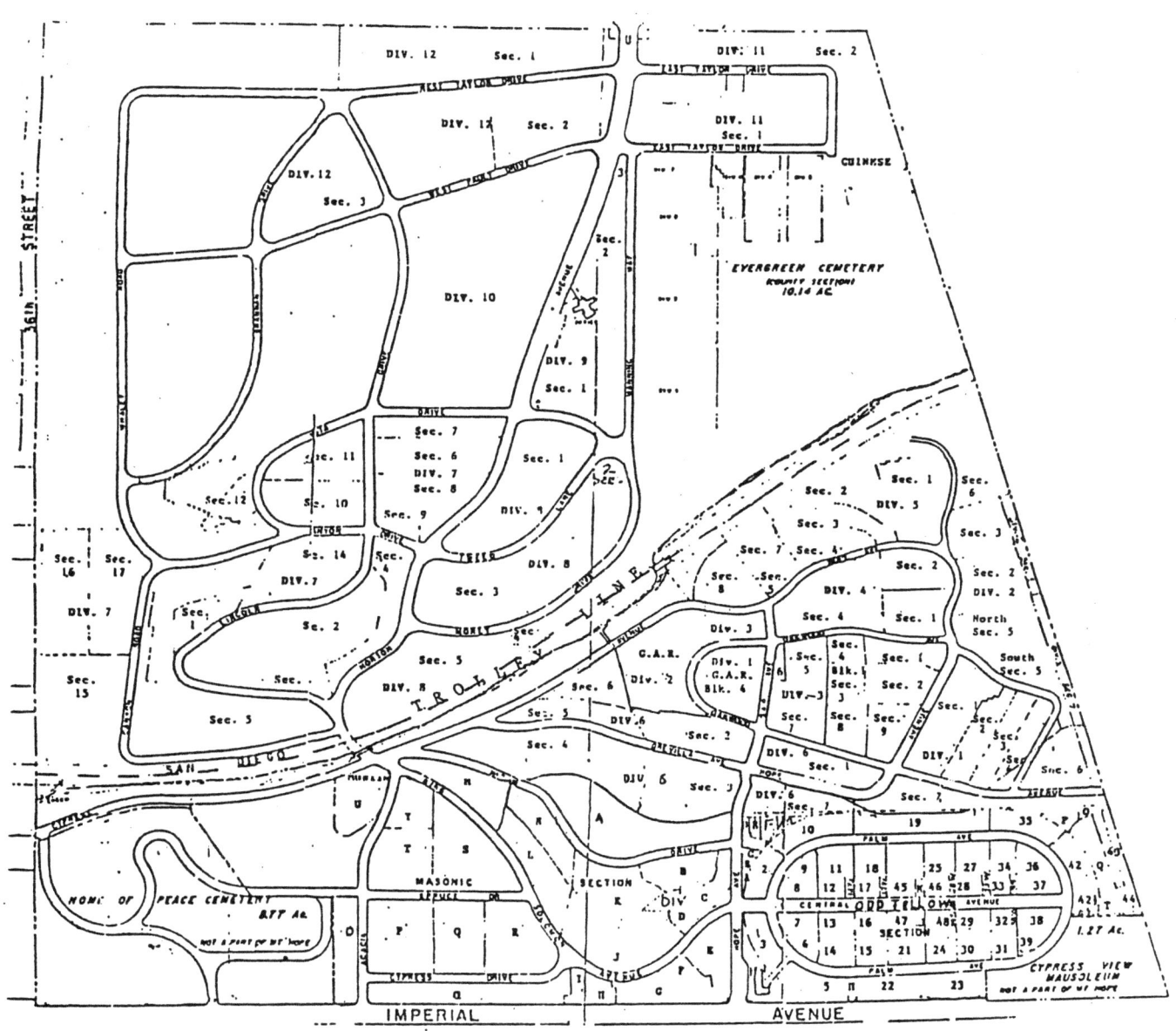

MOUNT HOPE CEMETERY

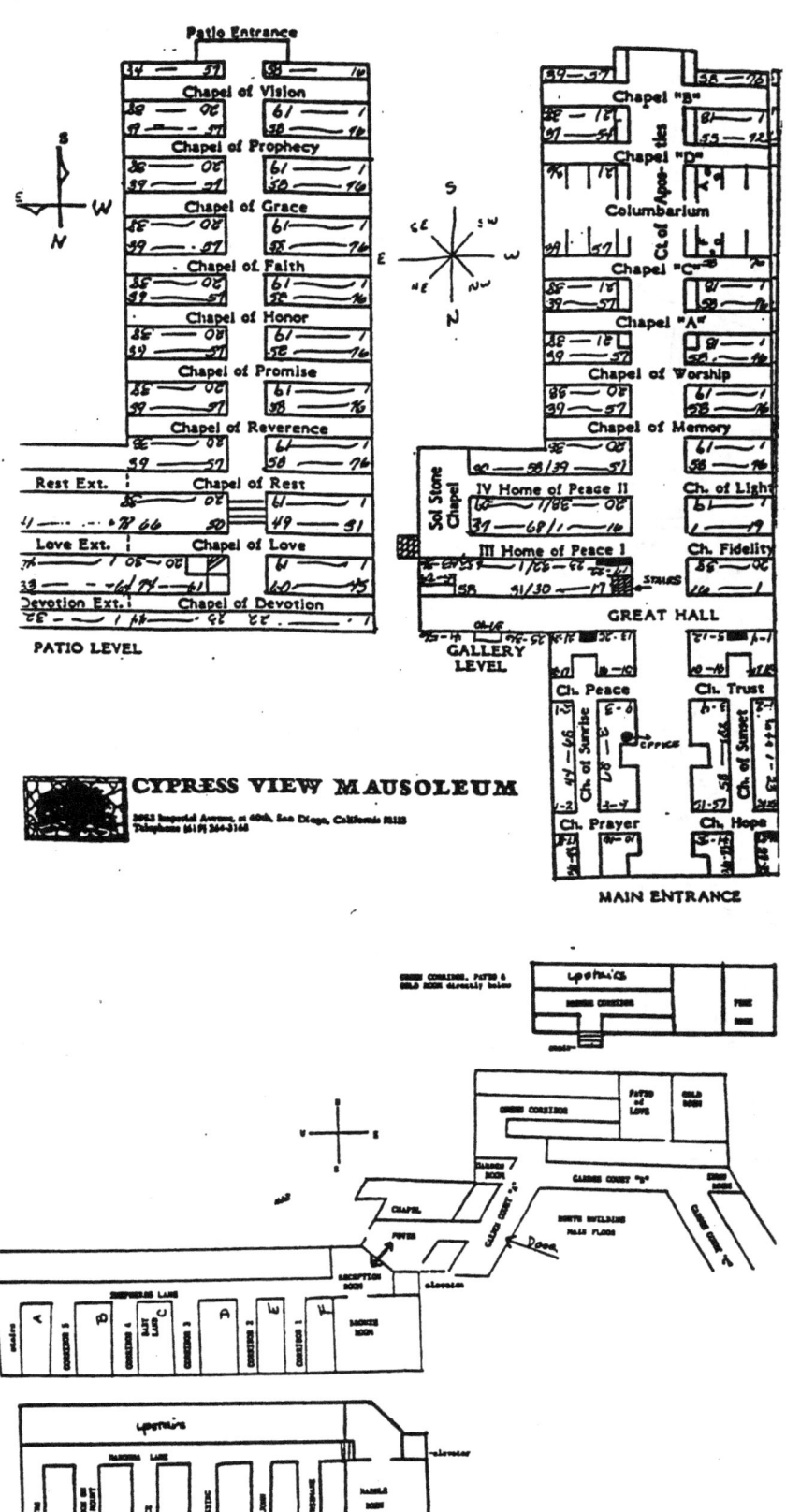

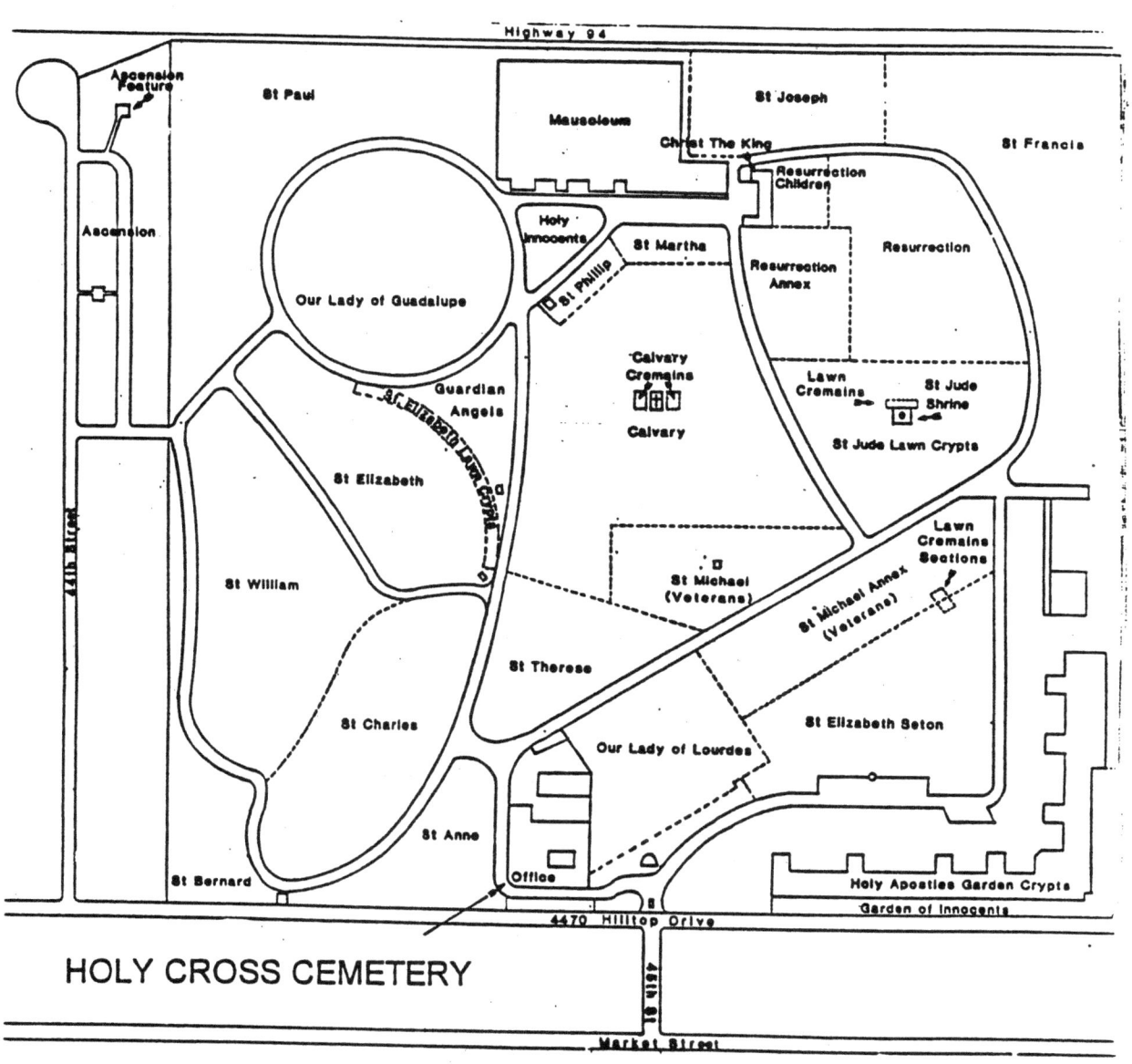

HOLY CROSS CEMETERY

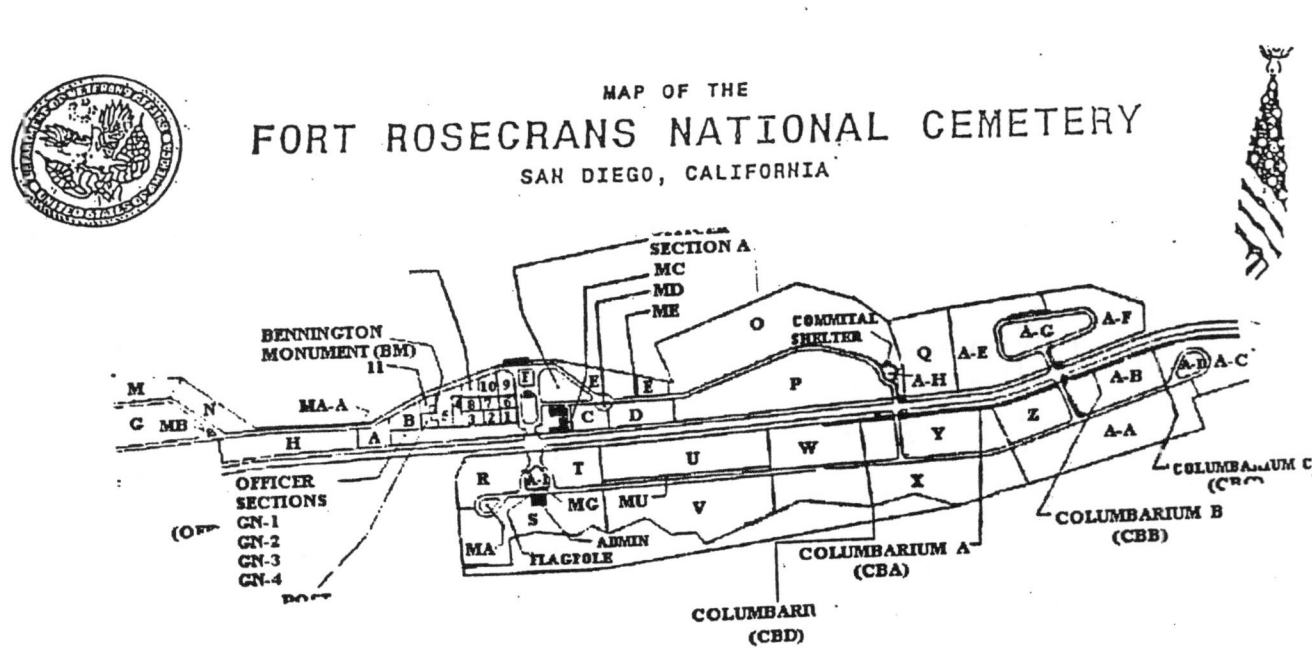